ns
THE GO
OLD TIME
Hockey
TRIVIA

DON WEEKES

GREYSTONE BOOKS
Douglas & McIntyre
VANCOUVER/TORONTO

For my mother, Dorothy, who inspired me to so many goals.

Copyright © 1997 by Don Weekes

97 98 99 00 01   5 4 3 2 1

All rights reserved. No part of this book may be reproduced, stored in a retrieval system or transmitted in any form or by any means, without the prior permission of the publisher or, in the case of photocopying or other reprographic copying, a licence from CANCOPY (Canadian Reprography Collective), Toronto, Ontario.

Greystone Books
A division of Douglas & McIntyre Ltd.
1615 Venables Street
Vancouver, British Columbia V5L 2H1

Canadian Cataloguing in Publication Data
Weekes, Don.
  The goal scorers

  ISBN 1-55054-571-X

  1. National Hockey League—Miscellanea. 2. Hockey—Miscellanea. I. Title.
GV847.8.N3W442 1997   796.962'64   C97-910390-8

Editing by Anne Rose and Kerry Banks
Cover and text design by Peter Cocking
Typesetting by DesignGeist
Front cover photograph courtesy of Frank Prazak/Hockey Hall of Fame
Back cover photograph courtesy of Hockey Hall of Fame
Printed and bound in Canada by Best Book Manufacturers

Every reasonable care has been taken to trace the ownership of copyrighted visual material. Information that will enable the publishers to rectify any reference or credit is welcome.

The publisher gratefully acknowledges the assistance of the Canada Council for the Arts and of the British Columbia Ministry of Tourism, Small Business and Culture.

Table of Contents

Preface	1
1. ICE BREAKERS	3
Answers	9
Game 1: Hall of Fame Nicknames	20
2. THE ROOKIES	22
Answers	26
Game 2: Rookie Snipers	36
3. REARGUARD GUNNERS	37
Answers	41
Game 3: Retired Numbers	51
4. THE GREAT ONE	52
Answers	56
Game 4: Team Goal-Leaders	62

5.	**RECORD BREAKERS**	**64**
	Answers	67
	Game 5: Evolution of a Record	74
6.	**THE BIG LINES**	**76**
	Answers	81
	Game 6: The Pinwheel Puzzle	92
7.	**MILESTONES**	**94**
	Answers	99
	Game 7: Games-Played Leaders	110
8.	**THE CHART TOPPERS**	**112**
	Answers	116
	Game 8: Old-Timer Totals	124
9.	**STANLEY CUP SHARPSHOOTERS**	**125**
	Answers	128
	Game Solutions	135
	Acknowledgements	140

PREFACE

More than a century ago, when the first stick-and-puck games were being played on rudimentary skates across the frozen lakes and rivers of Canada's frontier, the players of that time, like the players of today, were motivated by a simple and singular objective: to score goals. It was the basis of play. The sport at its essence.

From those humble beginnings came hockey's first heroes and champions. They barnstormed across the land, thrilling spectators with their speed and stickhandling virtuosity. Men such as Cyclone Taylor, Newsy Lalonde and Joe Malone soon became household names, and their goal-scoring exploits the stuff of legends.

Although hockey was a team sport, the glory often went to the individual. There were classic old-time goaltenders such as Georges Vezina and big-time bruising defensemen à la Eddie Shore, but the goal scorers became the greatest stars on the ice.

Howie Morenz was the first player to capture the imagination of the fan. His speed lifted crowds from their seats whenever his Flying Frenchmen played. He twice won the NHL scoring race and was named hockey's outstanding player of the first half-century. Then came the Conacher clan, the Bentley brothers and the two greatest players between 1945 and 1960, Maurice Richard and Gordie Howe.

Richard was the purest goal scorer the game had ever seen. Howe proved to be the complete player; his mythic strength and playmaking magic were revolutionary. Together, Richard and Howe brought competitive excellence to larger and larger audiences.

During the 1960s and 1970s, Bobby Hull, Phil Esposito, Bobby Orr and Guy Lafleur broke league records and new ground with their high-scoring, game-breaking styles. Hull refined the slap shot and made his the league's hardest; Esposito won five scoring titles as the consummate slot man; Orr literally transformed the defensive position; and Lafleur became the next torch-bearing sniper of the mighty Canadiens.

The puck was then passed to Wayne Gretzky, who changed the face of hockey through his brilliance on-ice and his contributions off it.

Among the superstars loomed other scoring talents: Lindsay, Béliveau, Sittler and Messier. Still others are remembered for their impact as the misfit record holder, the one-game wonder and the foot soldier who never got his acclaim.

The game has always been about scoring goals. There have been many great goalies and defensemen, but their main task was always to stop shooters and shots. In this book, we travel back in time to look at hockey's most astonishing goal- and point-scoring feats, and the immortals who wrote hockey history.

DON WEEKES
June 1997

Chapter ONE

ICE BREAKERS

While players in the late 1950s attempted to master the slap shot, Gordie Howe was reinventing that haphazard drive into a more controllable shot—the wrist slap shot. According to Howe: "The blade of the stick should come back waist high or higher on the backswing and should hit the puck clearly off the heel. I snap my wrists as I hit the puck." Howe's new shot worked so well that in 1962–63 he won the NHL scoring race and MVP status. Remarkably, he was in his 17th season and averaging 40 minutes of ice time per game—almost twice that of most NHL forwards—and outshooting and outskating players a decade younger. In this start-up chapter, we unwind a few slappers at some unlikely targets. The trick is to pick the multiple-choice answer that fits best. *(Answers are on page 9.)*

1.1 What is the highest goal count by one player in an NHL regular season?
A. 86 goals
B. 89 goals
C. 92 goals
D. 95 goals

1.2 Why was Bernie Geoffrion nicknamed "Boom-Boom"?
A. Because of his rugged checks
B. Because of his unpredictable temper
C. Because of his boisterous trash talk
D. Because of his thundering slap shot

1.3 **Which sniper scored the most points in the NHL's first 10 years?**
A. Joe Malone
B. Newsy Lalonde
C. Babe Dye
D. Cy Denneny

1.4 **As of 1996–97, how many NHLers have been inducted directly into the Hockey Hall of Fame without the usual three-year waiting period after retirement?**
A. One player, Gordie Howe
B. Two players
C. Four players
D. Eight players

1.5 **Who is the only NHL sniper to score a goal in every possible way in one game?**
A. Mario Lemieux
B. Bryan Trottier
C. Gordie Howe
D. Syl Apps

1.6 **What is the highest percentage of goals that one player has scored of his team's total goals in a season?**
A. 23 per cent
B. 33 per cent
C. 43 per cent
D. 53 per cent

1.7 **Who is the leading French-Canadian goal scorer in NHL history?**
A. Marcel Dionne
B. Henri Richard
C. Mike Bossy
D. Mario Lemieux

1.8 Who is No. 9 in the photo above? Even harder, who is the goalie he's crashed into?
A. Maurice Richard and Terry Sawchuk
B. Gordie Howe and Gump Worsley
C. Gordie Howe and Johnny Bower
D. Bobby Hull and Jacques Plante

1.9 What is the highest goal total for an NHL penalty-minute leader?
A. 20 goals
B. 25 goals
C. 30 goals
D. 35 goals

1.10 How many NHLers have recorded 30-goal, 300-penalty-minute seasons in league history? Name them.
A. One player
B. Three players
C. Five players
D. Seven players

1.11 As of 1997, which goal scorer is the longest-serving team captain of all time?
A. Montreal's Jean Béliveau
B. Detroit's Steve Yzerman
C. Boston's Dit Clapper
D. Toronto's George Armstrong

1.12 During a playoff game in the 1950s, which top scorer raised his stick towards the crowd and pretended to shoot it like a gun?
A. Detroit's Ted Lindsay
B. Boston's Fleming Mackell
C. Montreal's Henri Richard
D. New York's Andy Bathgate

1.13 Who was the most recent player to score *more than* five goals in an NHL game?
A. Darryl Sittler
B. Dave Andreychuk
C. Red Berenson
D. Mats Sundin

1.14 The four NHL snipers depicted in the baby pictures on the opposite page fall into which category?
A. Each grew up to win the NHL scoring race
B. Each grew up to win multiple Stanley Cups
C. Each grew up to become an MVP in the NHL
D. Each grew up to become a 50-goal scorer in the NHL

1.15 What is Hall of Famer Jean Béliveau's career record in the balloting for the Hart Trophy as league MVP?
A. Two Hart Trophies and four runner-up finishes
B. Three Hart Trophies and three runner-up finishes
C. Four Hart Trophies and two runner-up finishes
D. Six Hart Trophies

Who are the future superstars pictured here?

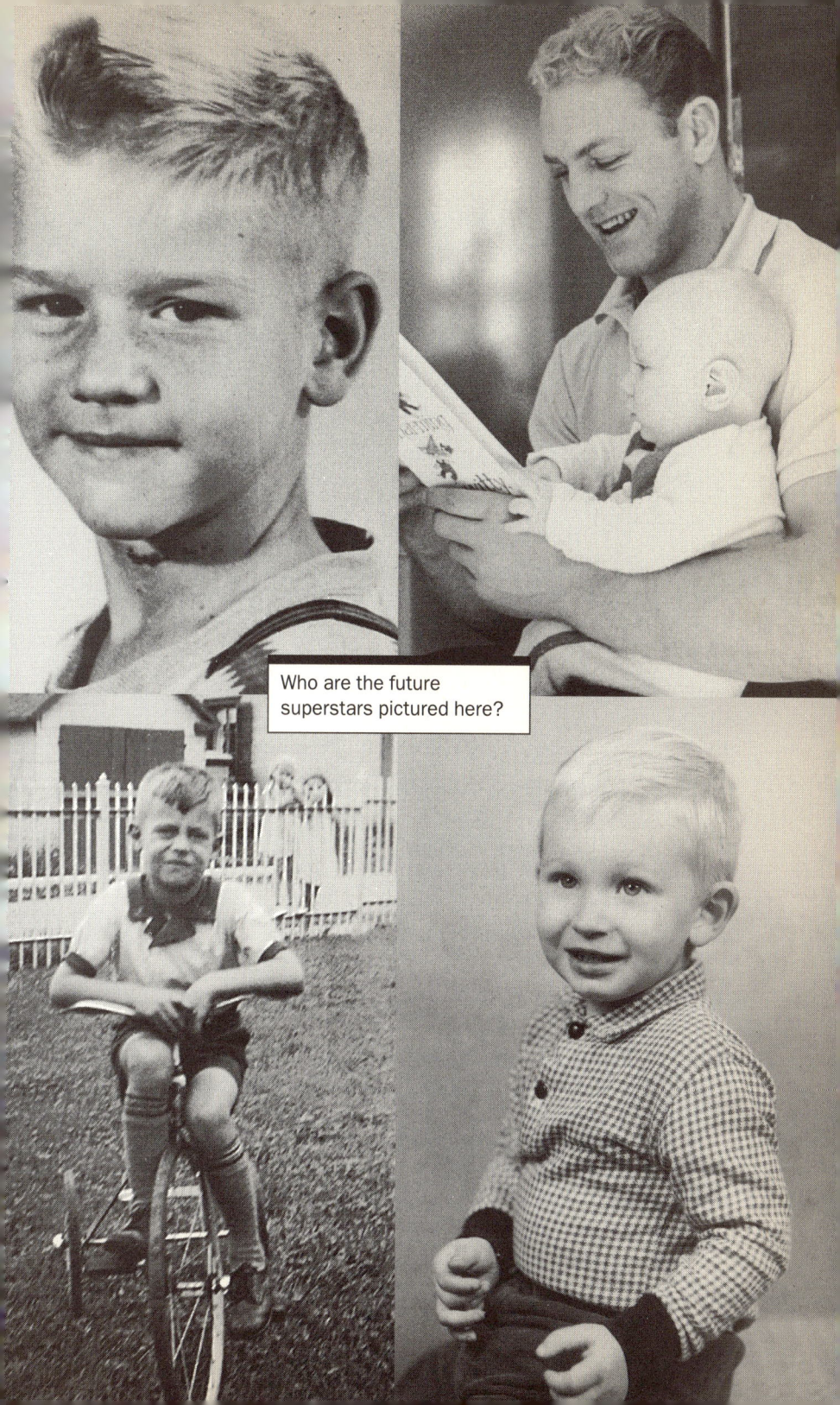

1.16 Who is the only NHL top 10 scorer to score 30 more goals than assists in a season?
A. Brett Hull
B. Maurice Richard
C. Teemu Selanne
D. Bill Cook

1.17 After Wayne Gretzky and Mario Lemieux, which player recorded the most points in his first four years in the NHL?
A. Mike Bossy
B. Peter Stastny
C. Howie Morenz
D. Milt Schmidt

1.18 Which jersey number has been worn most often by goal-scoring leaders?
A. No. 7
B. No. 9
C. No. 12
D. No. 16

1.19 Which old-time sniper was known as the "Big Bomber"?
A. Nels Stewart
B. Babe Dye
C. Bill Cook
D. Charlie Conacher

1.20 The Art Ross Trophy, the award presented annually to the NHL's top scorer, is named in honour of legendary Hall of Fame player, coach and general manager, Art Ross. How many goals did Ross score in the NHL?
A. One goal
B. Exactly 100 goals
C. Exactly 200 goals
D. Ross never played in the NHL

Answers

ICE BREAKERS

1.1 **C. 92 goals**
Old-time snipers say the pucks get bigger and the net gets smaller as the season wears on, but for Wayne Gretzky, in his youth, that particular hockey adage never applied. Gretzky was the proverbial Duracell bunny: he just kept going and going and going to score a mind-boggling 92 goals in 1981–82, his third NHL season. His favourite victims were Los Angeles' Mario Lessard, whom he netted seven goals against; and Hartford's Greg Millen, Philadelphia's Pete Peeters and Calgary's Reggie Lemelin, all of whom he beat five times.

1.2 **D. Because of his thundering slap shot**
When hockey writers of the 1950s first witnessed Geoffrion in practice slapping the puck with golf-swing shots, they called it a "slap" shot. Because of its inaccuracy and sheer velocity, pucks boomed off the boards, echoing across the rink. After that, Geoffrion became "Boom-Boom" and the slap shot joined the wrist shot and backhand shot as essential weapons in every scorer's arsenal.

1.3 **D. Cy Denneny**
During the NHL's first decade, 1917–18 to 1926–27, Denneny was the league's most prolific point earner, scoring 309 points with the old Ottawa Senators. His consistency was remarkable. With the exception of two seasons, the left-winger never dropped lower than third in league scoring in 10 years. Short, chunky Denneny had the scoring touch of all great players, plus the strength and tenacity of a pit bull. He was part goal scorer and part policeman, a lethal combination that kept his opponents honest and the Senators winning championships.

The NHL's First Decade Scoring Leaders (1917–18 to 1926–27)

Player	Team	GP	G	A	PTS
Cy Denneny	Ottawa	259	242	67	309
Babe Dye	Tor/Hamilton	211	201	41	242
Reg Noble	Tor/Mtl Maroons	260	144	55	199
Frank Nighbor	Ottawa	235	124	52	176
Joe Malone	Mtl/Que	125	146	18	164
Harry Broadbent	Ott/Mtl Maroons	215	118	39	157
George Boucher	Ottawa	259	108	44	152
Newsy Lalonde	Mtl/NY Americans	99	124	27	151

1.4 **C. Four players**

On only four occasions has the Hockey Hall of Fame invoked a special provision that allows it to waive the three-year waiting period after retirement, to immediately nominate players "of outstanding preeminence and skill" to the Hall. The NHL's first 20-year man, Dit Clapper, was inducted under such special status in 1947, just months after retiring from Boston. Gordie Howe and Jean Béliveau became instant Hall of Famers in 1972, the year of their retirements. In 1979, Bobby Orr went straight from the ice to hockey's hallowed Hall. The fifth individual inducted under those circumstances should be Mario Lemieux, who, at the time of this writing, had been nominated after his 1997 retirement.

1.5 **A. Mario Lemieux**

Lemieux is the only player to score a goal every possible way in the same game: at even strength, on the power play, shorthanded, on a penalty shot and into an empty net. It happened in Lemieux's first five-goal game on December 31, 1988, an 8–6 Pittsburgh win over New Jersey.

ICE BREAKERS: ANSWERS

1.6   C. 43 per cent

If you can appreciate how different the game is today compared to 20 years ago, imagine old-time hockey in 1919–20. That year, Quebec's Joe Malone won the NHL scoring race, netting 39 of his team's 91 goals in the 24-game schedule. With only 10 players on Quebec's roster, Malone played almost 60 minutes a game, typical ice time for that era. Goalie averages were laughable in the four-team NHL that season. Except for Ottawa's Clint Benedict (2.67), all other netminders averaged four or more goals per game. Ironically, the worst average came from Malone's own team. Quebec's goalies allowed 7.38 goals per game. Malone may own the NHL's best goals-on-a-team percentage, but his club finished 1919–20 with only four wins and 20 losses. The best percentage in the modern game belongs to Brett Hull, who scored 86 of St. Louis' 310 goals in 1990–91, about 28 per cent of his team's total goal output.

The NHL's Highest Goals-on-a-Team Percentage

Player	Team	Season	G	TG	PCT
Joe Malone	Quebec	1919–20	39	91	42.9
Babe Dye	Toronto	1924–25	38	90	42.2
Joe Malone	Montreal	1917–18	44	115	38.3
Nels Stewart	Maroons	1925–26	34	91	37.4
Cy Denneny	Ottawa	1917–18	36	102	35.3
Cy Denneny	Ottawa	1920–21	34	97	35.1
Bill Cook	Rangers	1926–27	33	95	34.7
Jimmy Herberts	Boston	1924–25	17	49	34.7

1.7   A. Marcel Dionne

It was obvious from the start that Dionne was destined to become another French-Canadian legend in the NHL.

Gilbert Perreault and Marcel Dionne. Two of French Canada's elite snipers of the 1970–80s.

ICE BREAKERS: ANSWERS

Born in Drummondville, Quebec, in 1951, Dionne was signing autographs in midget hockey. In the junior ranks, his scoring totals were almost unbelievable: 507 points in three years. At just five feet seven, Dionne was a whirling scoring machine who skated circles around most players. In 1971, Dionne was drafted second overall by Detroit, where he played four years and scored 366 points—more points in a four-year start than any other NHLer before him. His trade to Los Angeles in 1975 brought him to the Kings' Triple Crown Line and linemates Charlie Simmer and Dave Taylor. Dionne notched six 50-goal and seven 100-point years before finishing his career with the Rangers in 1989. In 18 NHL seasons, Dionne scored 731 goals and 1,771 points, third best behind only Wayne Gretzky and Gordie Howe in league history. Among all the greats to come out of Quebec, no one, including Maurice Richard, Guy Lafleur and Mario Lemieux, have put up numbers equal to Dionne's.

1.8 **B. Gordie Howe and Gump Worsley**
This photo resembles one of those find-the-puck tests. In this case, it's the two players' faces and identities we want. No. 9 is easy. Even though his head is turned away, it could only be Gordie Howe. The goalie? Almost impossible to tell. But if you look closely between Howe's left glove and shoulder, you'll see the unmistakable mug of Gump Worsley. The puck? Somewhere under Worsley, who stopped the shot and Howe on this play.

1.9 **D. 35 goals**
Quite a few players, including old-timers Maurice Richard and Ted Lindsay, have broken the 20-goal barrier while leading the NHL in penalty minutes. But no one touches Tiger Williams when it comes to combining box time and goal scoring. In 1980–81, Williams sat in the box for a league-high 343 minutes and still found time to score 35 goals for Vancouver.

THE GOAL SCORERS

Most Goals by Penalty-Minute Leaders*

Player	Team	Year	Goals	PIM
Tiger Williams	Vancouver	1980–81	35	343
Bob Probert	Detroit	1987–88	29	398
Maurice Richard	Montreal	1952–53	28	112
Ted Lindsay	Detroit	1958–59	22	184
John Ferguson	Montreal	1966–67	20	177
Dave Schultz	Philadelphia	1973–74	20	348

*Current to 1997

1.10 B. Three players

The 30-goal, 300-penalty-minute club is an exclusive fraternity. Many have tried to join, like Bob Probert, who just missed qualifying by one goal in 1987–88 with a 29–398 record. Obviously, it's a tough act to pull off: consistent goal scorer and resident policeman. So membership is limited and, so far, restricted to Tiger Williams, Al Secord and Rick Tocchet. No old-timer managed it until Williams, who founded the club in 1980–81 when he scored 35 goals and spent 343 minutes in the box. The following year, Secord came aboard with a 44–303 record. In 1987–88, Tocchet's 31 goals and 301 penalty minutes edged him nicely into the select group.

1.11 C. Boston's Dit Clapper

Clapper is the longest-serving NHL captain of all time. During the 1930s and 1940s, the Boston forward and defenseman meant as much to the team as Ray Bourque does today. Considered an athlete's athlete, Bourque dominated the game both on and off-ice with his size, power and scoring skills. Clapper, like Bourque, had a demeanour and grace that hockey seldom sees and teams seldom trade. Unlike Bourque, Clapper won three Stanley Cups with Boston during his 20-year career. He netted 221 goals and wore the "C" for 13 seasons over three terms: from 1932–33 to 1937–38, from 1939–40 to

1945–46, and in 1946–47 with John Crawford. Among active players in 1997, Bourque had captained or co-captained Boston for 12 seasons and Yzerman 11 years in Detroit. Armstrong spent 12 years (1957–58 to 1968–69) as Toronto's captain and Béliveau 10 years (1961–62 to 1970–71) in Montreal.

1.12 A. Detroit's Ted Lindsay
During the 1956 Red Wings–Maple Leafs semifinals, an anonymous caller, probably unhappy with Detroit's 2–0 series lead, telephoned Toronto newspapers threatening: "Don't worry about Howe and Lindsay tonight. I'm going to shoot them." Plainclothes policemen were assigned to watch the Wings and their two targeted players, who by game time were even more anxious, given all the publicity. Into the third period the threat seemed to be working. Detroit was down 4–2. But, as time ticked away, the mounting pressure fortified the Wings, and Howe and Lindsay each scored big goals to push the game into overtime. Then, at 4:22 of OT, Lindsay took a Bob Goldham pass at the Toronto goalmouth and whacked it beyond Leaf netminder Harry Lumley. After the game-winning goal, in defiance of the Toronto crowd, Lindsay raised the butt of his stick towards the stands and pretended to fire it like a gun. Lindsay's Hall of Fame career was defined by many such well-publicized events. He was one of old-time hockey's toughest and most feared players, yet he had league-wide respect as a goal scorer. He never backed down from anything or anyone: not his on-ice opponents, his team's management, league owners, and certainly not from disgruntled fans.

1.13 A. Darryl Sittler
Before 1967, only five players had scored more than five goals in a game. Since then, only two NHLers have hit the six-or-better plateau: St. Louis' Red Berenson recorded six goals on November 7, 1968, against Philadelphia in an 8–0 Blues win; Sittler, the most recent NHLer to manage a six-goal blitz, did it against Boston on February 7, 1976.

"Every time I had the puck, something seemed to happen," said Sittler. The Leaf forward also produced four assists in the 11–4 win, earning him a game total of 10 points, an NHL record. Interestingly, since Sittler scored his six goals split between the second and third periods, he became the first and only player to score hat tricks in consecutive periods of the same game. His victim, goalie Dave Reece, never played in the NHL again.

1.14 **C. Each grew up to become an MVP in the NHL**
The "baby" snipers are (clockwise from upper left): Bobby Orr, age six, in 1954; Brett Hull, age one, with superstar dad Bobby in 1965; Wayne Gretzky, age two, in 1963; and Jean Béliveau, age five, already with admirers in 1936. (The other multiple choices are incorrect because Hull has never won a scoring race or a Stanley Cup (as of 1997), and Orr never hit the 50-goal mark.)

1.15 **A. Two Hart Trophies and four runner-up finishes**
In a 14-year span, from 1956 to 1969, Béliveau was twice voted the league's most valuable player. But on another four occasions, the Canadiens' captain finished in the runner-up position. No MVP has ever come second so often. In one four-year period alone, Béliveau missed winning the Hart three times, losing to Bobby Hull in 1966, Stan Mikita in 1968 and Phil Esposito in 1969. That bit of trivia alone confirms Béliveau's greatness. By then, he was in the twilight of his stellar 18-year career.

1.16 **A. Brett Hull**
Considering the fact that today's top point-producers consistently score more assists than goals while old-time marksmen usually led the NHL points race by bulking up on goals, it's an oddity that the only NHLer ever to score 30 more goals than assists comes from the ranks of modern-day hockey. Bill Cook almost did it in 1926–27's 44-game schedule, when he scored 33 goals and four assists, and sometimes a player from today's game produces a 52-goal, 34-assist season like Keith Tkachuk's (1996–97), but

no one has done it with the frequency of Brett Hull. In three straight seasons, Hull netted either 41 or 31 more goals than assists: in 1989–90 (72-41-113), 1990–91 (86-45-131) and 1991–92 (70-39-109).

1.17 B. Peter Stastny

Gretzky and Lemieux scored 709 points and 516 points respectively during their first four NHL seasons. Trailing closely behind in third position is Stastny, the Quebec Nordique who amassed 491 points on four straight 100-point seasons between 1980 and 1984. Born in Czechoslovakia, Stastny defected to the Nordiques in 1980 and hit instant stardom, winning 1981's Calder Trophy as top NHL rookie.

The NHL's Best Four-Year Starts*

Player	Team	1st	2nd	3rd	4th	Total Points
Wayne Gretzky	Edm	137	164	212	196	709
Mario Lemieux	Pit	100	141	107	168	516
Peter Stastny	Que	109	139	124	119	491
Mike Bossy	NYI	91	126	92	119	428
Dale Hawerchuk	Wpg	103	91	102	130	426
Bryan Trottier	NYI	95	72	123	134	424
Denis Savard	Chi	75	119	121	94	409

*Current to 1997

1.18 B. No. 9

No jersey number in hockey is more famous than No. 9. It has been worn by many goal-scoring leaders, such as Charlie Conacher, Lynn Patrick, Maurice Richard, Gordie Howe and Bobby Hull. No. 7 has also been popular, used by Howie Morenz, Ted Lindsay, Bobby Hull (one season), Norm Ullman and Phil Esposito. Another favourite is No. 12, used by Gordie Drillon, Bryan Hextall, Sid Abel, Dickie Moore and Peter Bondra.

1.19 D. Charlie Conacher
Standing two inches taller and weighing 20 pounds heavier than the average player of his era, Conacher dominated the game in the 1930s, not only with his size and strength but with his hustle and heavy shot. His shooting terrorized goalies and made him the league's goal-scoring champ five times, the winner of two NHL scoring crowns and a five-time All-Star. The "Big Bomber" scored more than most of his contemporaries, but not without linemates Busher Jackson and Joe Primeau. They became Toronto's number one scoring unit, best remembered as The Kid Line. Conacher played 12 NHL seasons—nine of them in Toronto.

1.20 A. One goal
Scoring is one of the few aspects of hockey that Art Ross did not have a large impact on, which is ironic considering that the annual award for the NHL's top scorer bears his name. Ross invented the B-shaped goal net and the helmet, improved the sliding action of the puck and also served as an NHL referee, coach and general manager. Ross, a defenseman, played only three games in the NHL, scoring exactly one goal. He scored it on December 19, 1917, the NHL's first night of operation, against goalie Sammy Herbert of Toronto. Ross was a member of the Montreal Wanderers, one of four teams that composed the NHL in its inaugural season in 1917–18. Because several star players were absent from their teams, some players, who would not have been on the roster a year earlier in the NHA, were on the benches for this first game. Ross belonged to this category. He was "a substitute who went in only at times to rest the other men," according to local papers at the time. Ross scored on his first shift at 17:30 of the second period. The Wanderers withdrew from the NHL after just six games when their home rink burned down on January 2, 1918, and Ross retired with one NHL goal to his credit. He did, however, score 84 goals in his 12-year pro career prior to the formation of the NHL, and won Stanley Cups as a player in 1907 and 1908.

Charles Conacher. The Big Bomber was a five-time NHL goal-scoring leader.

Game ONE

HALL OF FAME NICKNAMES

When Howie Morenz launched himself on his patented headlong rushes down the ice, it was with full-speed recklessness, a wild abandonment that dazzled spectators, awed opponents and earned him a variety of nicknames: "Stratford Streak," "Canadien Comet," "Hurtling Habitant" and "The Mitchell Meteor." Morenz, the game's first true superstar, collected the most nicknames of any sniper in NHL history. Yet perhaps his most deserving moniker, penned by American sportswriters, was "The Babe Ruth of Hockey."

In this game, match the Hall of Famers (and would-be Famers) with their famous nicknames. *(Solutions are on page 135)*

Part 1

1. _____ Maurice Richard   A. "The Roadrunner"
2. _____ Eric Lindros   B. "J. R."
3. _____ Lionel Conacher   C. "Little Beaver"
4. _____ Marcel Dionne   D. "The Rocket"
5. _____ Aurel Joliat   E. "Chief"
6. _____ Mike Bossy   F. "The Big Train"
7. _____ Yvan Cournoyer   G. "Butch"
8. _____ Johnny Bucyk   H. "The Mighty Atom"
9. _____ Emile Bouchard   I. "Boss"
10. _____ Jeremy Roenick   J. "The Next One"

Part 2

1. _____ Mark Messier   A. "The Russian Rocket"
2. _____ Cecil Dye   B. "Boom-Boom"
3. _____ Pavel Bure   C. "Babe"
4. _____ Frank Nighbor   D. "Teeder"
5. _____ Bernie Geoffrion   E. "Le Magnifique"
6. _____ Ted Kennedy   F. "Busher"
7. _____ Guy Lafleur   G. "Moose"
8. _____ Gordie Howe   H. "The Flying Dutchman"
9. _____ Harvey Jackson   J. "Flower"
10. _____ Mario Lemieux   I. "Mr. Hockey"

Part 3
1. _____Bobby Hull
2. _____Jaromir Jagr
3. _____Alex Delvecchio
4. _____Hector Blake
5. _____Brett Hull
6. _____Nels Stewart
7. _____Max Bentley
8. _____Henri Richard
9. _____Fred Taylor
10. _____Eddie Shore

A. "The Golden Brett"
B. "The Pocket Rocket"
C. "Old Poison"
D. "Fats"
E. "The Edmonton Express"
F. "Toe"
G. "The Human Highlight Reel"
I. "The Golden Jet"
H. "Cyclone"
J. "The Dipsy-Doodle Dandy of Delisle."

Part 4
1. _____Wayne Gretzky
2. _____Frank Mahovlich
3. _____Larry Robinson
4. _____Mel Hill
5. _____Reggie Leach
6. _____Jack Stewart
7. _____Pierre Larouche
8. _____Bryan Trottier
9. _____Edouard Lalonde
10. _____Jean Béliveau

A. "Black Jack"
B. "Lucky Pierre"
C. "The Rifle"
D. "The Great One"
E. "The Big M"
F. "Le Gros Bill"
G. "Big Bird"
H. "Newsy"
I. "Trots"
J. "Sudden Death"

Chapter TWO

THE ROOKIES

Since the NHL began in 1917–18, only 35 players have scored five goals in a game. Has a rookie ever uncorked five goals in 60 minutes? Yes—twice. Toronto's Howie Meeker scored five times against Chicago on January 8, 1947, in his freshman year; and rookie Don Murdoch of the Rangers posted a five-goal game on October 12, 1976, in a 10–4 rout of Minnesota.

(Answers are on page 26)

2.1 What is the record for most goals by a player in his first NHL game?
  A. One goal
  B. Two goals
  C. Three goals
  D. Four goals

2.2 How many goals did Steve Yzerman score as a rookie?
  A. More than Guy Lafleur in his rookie season
  B. More than Steve Larmer in his rookie season
  C. More than Luc Robitaille in his rookie season
  D. More than Dale Hawerchuk in his rookie season

2.3 Who was the last rookie to be traded midway through the year he won the Calder Trophy?
  A. Ed Litzenberger, in 1955
  B. Roger Crozier, in 1965
  C. Eric Vail, in 1975
  D. It has never happened

THE ROOKIES: QUESTIONS

2.4 **What is the record for goals by a rookie defenseman?**
A. 23 goals
B. 25 goals
C. 27 goals
D. 29 goals

2.5 **How long did Bernie Geoffrion's 1951–52 rookie record of 30 goals in a season last?**
A. One year
B. Five to 10 years
C. 10 to 15 years
D. More than 15 years

2.6 **How many rookies have scored 100-or-more point seasons in their NHL debut? Name them, too.**
A. Three rookies
B. Five rookies
C. Seven rookies
D. Nine rookies

2.7 **How many rookies have won an NHL goal-scoring race?**
A. None
B. One rookie
C. Three rookies
D. Five rookies

2.8 **Who is the youngest NHL player to score 100 points in a season?**
A. Mario Lemieux
B. Jimmy Carson
C. Wayne Gretzky
D. Dale Hawerchuk

2.9 **What jersey number was Gordie Howe wearing when he scored his first NHL goal in 1946?**
A. No. 7
B. No. 17
C. No. 27
D. Howe has always worn No. 9

2.10 **What is the record for most points accumulated by a player in his first NHL game?**
A. Three points
B. Four points
C. Five points
D. Six points

2.11 **Who was the first NHL rookie to post a 50-goal season?**
A. Rick Martin
B. Mike Bossy
C. Mario Lemieux
D. Joe Nieuwendyk

2.12 **What is the shortest amount of time it has taken for an NHL rookie of the year to prove himself by winning the NHL scoring race?**
A. One season
B. Two seasons
C. Three seasons
D. Four seasons

2.13 **Since the NHL took sole ownership of the Stanley Cup in 1927, who is the only rookie to score a Stanley Cup-winning goal?**
A. Montreal's Howie Morenz, in 1930
B. Boston's Roy Conacher, in 1939
C. Toronto's Howie Meeker, in 1947
D. Chicago's Ab McDonald, in 1961

2.14 **Who is the future NHL rookie of the year on the opposite page?**
A. Howie Meeker
B. Frank Mahovlich
C. Dave Keon
D. Kent Douglas

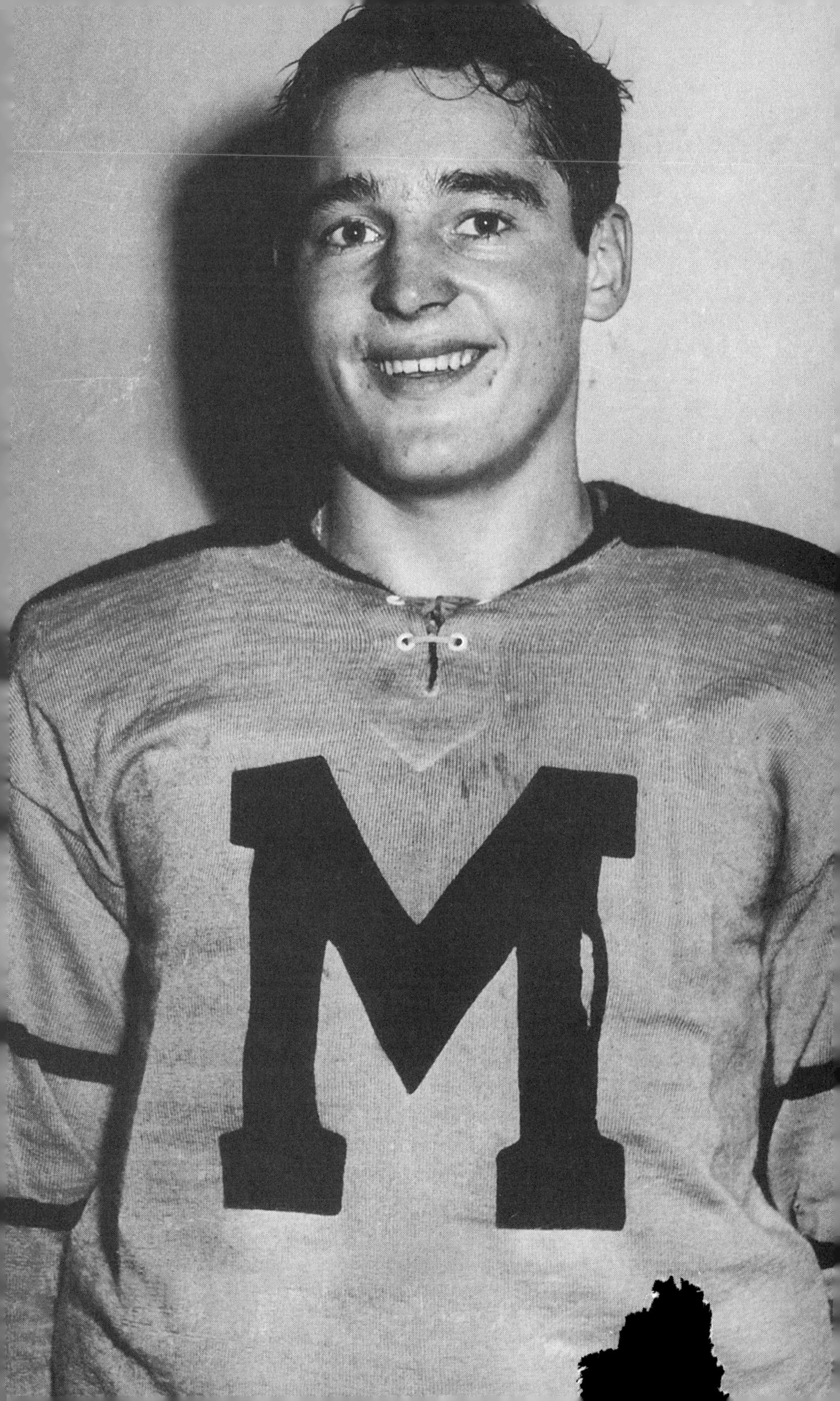

Answers

THE ROOKIES

2.1 **C. Three goals**
Two rookies are tied for this goal-scoring record, and they couldn't be further apart in experience. Réal Cloutier, a two-time WHA scoring champion, wasted no time after landing in the NHL, recording a hat trick in his first NHL game on October 10, 1979. Thirty-five years earlier, on January 14, 1943, Alex Smart, an unknown forward from Brandon, Manitoba, stepped onto Montreal Forum ice for his first match and scored three times. While Cloutier's NHL career lasted six seasons and 344 points, Smart's scoring touch quickly faded: seven games later he was on the train home. Of some consolation, Smart's hat trick did earn Montreal a 5–1 win over Chicago, but Cloutier's goals were in vain; Quebec lost to Atlanta 5–3.

2.2 **A. More than Guy Lafleur in his rookie season**
Yzerman made a big impression in his rookie season, scoring 39 goals for Detroit in 1983–84. The only rookie from our All-Star group of Lafleur, Hawerchuk and Robitaille who scored fewer goals in his first season is Lafleur, who counted a respectable 29 goals in 1971–72. Robitaille (45), Hawerchuk (45) and Larmer (43) all outscored Yzerman in their inaugural NHL campaigns.

2.3 **A. Ed Litzenberger, in 1955**
During the 1950s, Chicago was in a desperate situation. The floundering Blackhawks literally lived in the league basement with nine last-place finishes in 11 seasons. Attendance had dropped to 4,500 per game. To beef up the Hawks roster, the NHL asked teams to release almost a dozen players. In midseason, the Canadiens

dealt Litzenberger to Chicago for a waiver price. Chicago finished last again, but Litzenberger's hard shot and smooth skating earned him the Calder as top rookie. His 51 points on 23 goals and 28 assists ranked 12th best among all NHLers. Montreal's loss of Litzenberger had little bearing on its success. Montreal won five Stanley Cups between 1956 and 1960. Litzenberger, who played in a record 73 games during 1954–55's 70-game schedule (29 games in Montreal and 44 in Chicago), eventually won championships in Chicago in 1961 and Toronto in 1962, 1963 and 1964.

2.4 **A. 23 goals**
By the end of 1988–89, the Rangers knew that their first-round draft pick of 1986 had not been wasted on just another overrated star college player. Brian Leetch quickly demonstrated that his electrifying raw talent had impact at the NHL level. His hard, accurate shot and superior defensive skills made him a game-breaking defenseman of the calibre of Bobby Orr and Ray Bourque. His creativity as a playmaker and scorer was almost scary. In 1988–89, Leetch won the Calder Trophy as rookie of the year, setting an NHL record for goals (23) by a rookie defenseman.

2.5 **D. More than 15 years**
Among the many French-Canadian superstars to come out of the fabled Montreal Canadiens dressing room during the dynasty years of the 1950s, few, with the exception of Jean Béliveau and Maurice and Henri Richard, could compare in spirit or shooting skill to Geoffrion. Forever in their shadow, Geoffrion had to be content with being the number-three star forward (almost as Ron Francis was to Mario Lemieux and Jaromir Jagr in Pittsburgh). With any other team, Geoffrion would have been a franchise player. On the talent-rich Canadiens, he was expected to be great, but was not honoured for his greatness. When he won the NHL scoring race in 1954–55, Montreal fans booed him long and loud for "stealing" the scoring title

from the suspended Maurice Richard. Among the Habs' historic jersey numbers, Geoffrion's No. 5 is still not retired by the club. Yet he won two scoring titles, five Stanley Cups and was the second NHLer to score 50 goals in a season. Perhaps his greatest scoring feat came in his rookie year when he scored an eye-popping 30 goals, a record that stood for 17 seasons, until Danny Grant and Norm Ferguson ripped 34 goals in 1968–69.

2.6 **B. Five rookies**

Considering the magnitude of the achievement, 100 or more rookie points, it's remarkable that even five players reached such scoring heights as freshmen. It's particularly amazing when you look down the list of those stars (many of them future Hall of Famers) who came close with 90 or more points.

The NHL's All-Time Top Point-Scoring Rookies*

Player	Team	Season	GP	G	A	PTS
Teemu Selanne	Wpg	1992–93	84	76	56	132
Peter Stastny	Que	1980–81	77	39	70	109
Dale Hawerchuk	Wpg	1981–82	80	45	58	103
Joe Juneau	Bos	1992–93	84	32	70	102
Mario Lemieux	Pit	1984–85	73	43	57	100
Neal Broten	Min	1981–82	73	38	60	98
Bryan Trottier	NYI	1975–76	80	32	63	95
Barry Pederson	Bos	1981–82	80	44	48	92
Joe Nieuwendyk	Cal	1987–88	75	51	41	92
Mike Bossy	NYI	1977–78	73	53	38	91
Steve Larmer	Chi	1982–83	80	43	47	90

*Current to 1997

2.7 **C. Three rookies**

A number of old-time players (Babe Dye, Charlie Conacher, Gord Drillon and Cooney Weiland) won goal-scoring titles in their second seasons, but only three players in NHL history have done it as rookies. The Montreal Maroons' Nels Stewart established his scoring might in 1925–26, firing a league-high 34 goals to become the first NHL freshman to win a goal-scoring race and a scoring title (42 points). In 1938–39, Boston Bruins rookie Roy Conacher scored 26 goals to top the goal-scorers' list. In 1992–93, the Winnipeg Jets' Teemu Selanne became the third rookie to lead the NHL in goals, tying Alexander Mogilny with 76.

2.8 D. Dale Hawerchuk

As of 1997, only four teenagers have recorded 100-point seasons in the NHL. Gretzky, Lemieux, Carson and Hawerchuk all qualify, but Hawerchuk was the youngest. At age 18, he scored 45 goals and 58 assists for 103 points with the Winnipeg Jets in 1981–82. Hawerchuk was an easy first-round draft choice (first overall) for the Jets in 1981. Thanks to his sterling offensive play, the Cornwall Royals won back-to-back Memorial Cups in 1980 and 1981, and Hawerchuk was named the Canadian Major Junior Player of the Year and the QMJHL Player of the Year in 1981. In his final season with the Royals, Hawerchuk scored an amazing 81 goals and 183 points. No question, he was primed for the NHL.

The NHL's Youngest 100-Point Scorers*

Player	Team	Year	G	A	PTS	Age
Dale Hawerchuk	Wpg	1981–82	45	58	103	18.11
Wayne Gretzky	Edm	1979–80	51	86	137	19.2
Mario Lemieux	Pit	1984–85	43	57	100	19.6
Jimmy Carson	LA	1987–88	55	52	107	19.8
Pierre Larouche	Pit	1975–76	53	58	111	20.4
Pierre Turgeon	Buf	1989–90	40	66	106	20.7
Joe Sakic	Que	1989–90	39	63	102	20.8
Rob Brown	Pit	1988–89	49	66	115	20.11

*Current to 1997

Gordie Howe. Hockey's most famous No. 9.

2.9 **B. No. 17**
Howe's career spanned an astonishing five decades, or 32 seasons, from 1946 to 1980. So incredible was his longevity that his totals, such as 2,421 NHL and WHA games played, are almost incomprehensible. Howe wore his famous No. 9 jersey in all but two seasons, 1946–47 and 1947–48. His only other sweater number was No. 17, which he wore when he scored his first goal in his first game on October 16, 1946. "It started in Omaha because

THE ROOKIES: ANSWERS

I was 17 years of age, so I became No. 17 up here," Howe recalls. "But then the trainer came to me and said, '(Roy) Conacher just got traded to New York. No. 9 is open. Do you want it?' I said, 'No.' He said, 'It'll get you a lower berth on the train.' I said, 'I'll take it.'"

2.10 **C. Five points**
Al Hill played 221 games and scored 95 points during eight NHL seasons with Philadelphia, but nothing compared to his first match on February 14, 1977. Hill scored two goals on his first two shots and added three assists to set an NHL rookie record of five points in the 6–4 Flyers win over St. Louis. The 21-year-old from the American Hockey League took just 36 seconds to score with a 45-foot blast past the Blues' Yves Belanger. A number of other rookies—Alex Smart, Earl Reibel and Roland Eriksson—have recorded four points in their first game, but none have matched Hill's 1977 five-pointer.

2.11 **B. Mike Bossy**
You've heard of the scorer's touch? Mike Bossy had it in spades. His feel for a hockey stick was so precise that he'd send the sticks he ordered back to the manufacturer if they were an ounce too heavy. Bossy exhibited the same precision with his shot: not only did he get it away quickly, it was incredibly accurate. In his rookie season with the New York Islanders in 1977–78, Bossy fired 53 goals behind opposition netminders. No other NHL rookie had ever scored so many goals. The dreaded sophomore jinx held no terror for Bossy. The next year, he rifled in 69 goals to establish a new single-season record for right-wingers.

2.12 **A. One season**
No top NHL rookie has ever won the league scoring race. Of course, you have to exclude Wayne Gretzky, who might have pulled it off had he not been twice discredited in 1979–80. First, for not being considered a rookie in his first NHL season (though, his WHA records don't officially

count towards his pro point totals), and second, for tying Marcel Dionne in points, but losing the scoring title because Dionne scored more goals (even though goals and assists are worth the same). Calder Trophy winners such as Bobby Orr (1967), Bryan Trottier (1976) and Mario Lemieux (1985) all played three seasons before winning their respective scoring championships in 1970, 1979 and 1988. But a lesser-known rookie of the year took the scoring title in his sophomore season. (Before the Calder Trophy was first awarded in 1937, the league elected its top freshman in name only, starting in 1933.) The New York Americans' Sweeney Schriner won rookie-of-the-year honours with the eighth-best scoring record (18–22–40) in 1934–35, and followed through in 1935–36 with a league-high 19–26–45 in the 48-game schedule. Schriner was a big winger, both fast and nimble. He won a second straight scoring title in 1936–37. But his greatest fame came as a Maple Leaf during the Stanley Cup finals of 1942, when he scored five goals. Down three games to Detroit, the Leafs battled back in hockey's most famous come-from-behind series. A packed Maple Leaf Gardens watched Schriner score twice to give Toronto a 3–1 win and the championship in the seventh and deciding game. Schriner is a member of the Hockey Hall of Fame.

2.13 **B. Boston's Roy Conacher, in 1939**
Younger sibling of the famous Hall of Fame Conachers, Lionel and Charlie, brother Roy started his NHL career in grand fashion, scoring a league-high 26 goals in his freshman year, 1938–39. It was only the second time a rookie has led the NHL in goals. In the playoffs, Conacher played even better, notching six goals, including five in the finals, still an NHL rookie record. To cap off his Cinderella story, the Bruins won the Stanley Cup on Conacher's Cup winner, on April 16, 1939. Few rookies ever get as much ice time as he did during those playoffs, but after his stellar debut, Conacher was handed a regular shift on Boston's second line with Bill Cowley and Mel Hill. According to

Sweeney Schriner won two scoring titles with the New York Americans before his trade to Toronto.

Roy Conacher was a rookie sensation in 1939.

the local papers, "Conacher's winning goal was the prettiest thing of the night. [Eddie] Shore started it at his defense by passing to Cowley, who skidded the puck across the ice when checked at the Toronto defense. Conacher, flying like the wind, took it in stride and hung the rubber behind [Turk] Broda with 18 minutes of the second period gone."

2.14 **B. Frank Mahovlich**
There was little surprise when Mahovlich won the Calder Trophy as top rookie in 1958. He was a star even before he joined the NHL, winning the OHA Junior A MVP Award with St. Michael's in Toronto (as seen in the picture). His impact as an offensive player was felt wherever he played during his 17-year NHL career. Mahovlich had a smooth-skating, effortless style that he displayed as he swooped into the opponent's zone to fire a cannonading blast. He helped the Leafs to four Stanley Cups; Montreal to two Cups; and Gordie Howe, his Detroit linemate, to his first 100-point season in 1968–69. Mahovlich's best NHL season was in 1971–72, when he scored 96 points as a Canadien.

Game TWO

ROOKIE SNIPERS

Listed below are the first names of some of hockey's top scoring rookies. Once you've figured out their last names, find them in the puzzle by reading across, down or diagonally. Following our example of Mike B-O-S-S-Y, connect the other 20 names using letters no more than once. Start with the letters printed in heavy type.

(Solutions are on page 136)

Joe _____	Luc _____	Neal _____	Gil _____
Dale _____	Ray _____	Eric _____	Rick _____
Peter _____	Eric _____	Mario _____	Steve _____
Steve _____	Teemu _____	Barry _____	Warren _____
Pierre _____	Darryl _____	Anton _____	Mikael _____

```
A Y N R E N B S E
M N L T R E T I S U
R R A G S A M H T X
E M N D R E E L A E
Z R E O L A P P U R
Y N A V S N U T Y R
E L I R Y I S T N E
T O R E S E R E T P
E B N D K S U S A T
O G I E P Y O W G S
N R T A N N D B E N
U S L R R H E N O U
T E O R A O A E L Y
S I N D H M B W I L
L K U C R E I T A
```

Chapter THREE

REARGUARD GUNNERS

Do any NHL defensemen currently hold their team's record for career points? Surprisingly, the answer is two: Al MacInnis of Calgary and Ray Bourque of Boston. MacInnis amassed a Flames record of 822 points on 213 goals and 606 assists in his 13 years in Cowtown. Bourque became the Bruins' all-time leading scorer when he surpassed Johnny Bucyk's career total of 1,339 points during the 1996–97 season. In this chapter, we toast (and roast) some of hockey's most outstanding offensive defensemen. *(Answers are on page 41)*

3.1 **Which defenseman scored the most points in his rookie season?**
   A. New York's Brian Leetch
   B. Calgary's Gary Suter
   C. Boston's Ray Bourque
   D. Los Angeles' Larry Murphy

3.2 **If Wayne Gretzky's 51-game consecutive point-scoring streak is the NHL record for all skaters, what is the longest point-scoring streak for a defenseman? Name the record holder, too.**
   A. 18 games
   B. 28 games
   C. 38 games
   D. 48 games

3.3 Who is the only defenseman to win the Hart Trophy as league MVP four times?
A. Eddie Shore
B. Bobby Orr
C. Red Kelly
D. Paul Coffey

3.4 How many goals did Bobby Orr score in his best offensive season?
A. 38 goals
B. 42 goals
C. 46 goals
D. 50 goals

3.5 What is the record for most goals by a defenseman in one season?
A. 46 goals
B. 48 goals
C. 50 goals
D. 52 goals

3.6 Considering the NHL was formed in 1917–18, in what year did a defenseman first record a 20-goal season? Name the D-man, too.
A. 1917–18
B. 1924–25
C. 1934–35
D. 1944–45

3.7 Which defenseman amassed the longest consecutive point-scoring streak in playoff action?
A. Montreal's Doug Harvey
B. Boston's Bobby Orr
C. Calgary's Al MacInnis
D. Detroit's Red Kelly

3.8 Who was the first defenseman drafted first overall since the NHL Amateur Draft began in 1969?
A. Rick Green

B. Greg Joly
C. Denis Potvin
D. Larry Robinson

3.9 Who is the only defenseman in NHL history to record a five-goal game?
A. Toronto's King Clancy
B. Calgary's Gary Suter
C. Montreal's J. C. Tremblay
D. Toronto's Ian Turnbull

3.10 Which defenseman's record for most points in a season did Bobby Orr break in 1968–69?
A. Chicago's Pierre Pilote
B. Detroit's Red Kelly
C. Montreal's Doug Harvey
D. Toronto's Tim Horton

3.11 Who was the first defenseman to score six assists in a game?
A. Babe Pratt
B. Tom Johnson
C. Lionel Conacher
D. Babe Siebert

3.12 What is the record for most goals scored by two defensemen (as teammates or as opponents) in one game?
A. Four goals
B. Six goals
C. Eight goals
D. 10 goals

3.13 In what season did Bobby Orr become the first defenseman in NHL annals to win the scoring race?
A. 1968–69
B. 1969–70
C. 1970–71
D. 1971–72

3.14 **How many NHL defensemen have recorded 100-or-more-point seasons?**
  A. Two D-men: Bobby Orr and Paul Coffey
  B. Three D-men: Bobby Orr, Paul Coffey and Brian Leetch
  C. Four D-men
  D. Five D-men

3.15 **Which defenseman was the first skater (non-goalie) in NHL history to win the Calder Trophy as top rookie and a first team All-Star berth in the same season?**
  A. Denis Potvin
  B. Bobby Orr
  C. Ray Bourque
  D. Jacques Laperriere

Answers

REARGUARD GUNNERS

3.1 **D. Los Angeles' Larry Murphy**

Among the NHL's top point-earning defensemen, Murphy has gone quietly about his job since 1980–81, working hard on defense, leading attacks and directing power plays. He is one of the many offensive-minded D-men to come along and make his scoring presence known since Bobby Orr, but Murphy was never as conspicuous as Ray Bourque, Brian Leetch or Chris Chelios. The exception might be Murphy's rookie year, 1980–81, when he grabbed the spotlight with his startling 76-point season to break the freshman mark held by Bourque (65 points). It has not been equalled by any first-year rearguard since Murphy's record of 16-60-76 powered the Kings to a second-place finish in the Norris Division and helped the Triple Crown Line of Marcel Dionne, Dave Taylor and Charlie Simmer to its best season ever. Murphy was runner-up to Quebec's Peter Stastny in Calder Trophy voting as top rookie.

The NHL's Top Point-Scoring Rookie Defensemen*

Player	Team	Season	G	A	PTS
Larry Murphy	Los Angeles	1980–81	16	60	76
Brian Leetch	NYR	1988–89	23	48	71
Gary Suter	Calgary	1985–86	18	50	68
Phil Housley	Buffalo	1982–83	19	47	66
Ray Bourque	Boston	1979–80	17	48	65
Chris Chelios	Montreal	1984–85	9	55	64

*Current to 1997

Eddie Shore. The original Big Bad Bruin.

3.2 **B. 28 games**

Considering the magnitude of Gretzky's 51-game scoring streak, it's difficult to imagine anyone coming close to his mark, except Mario Lemieux (46 games) or Gretzky himself (39 games). Mats Sundin managed a 30-game streak in 1992–93 and supersnipers Steve Yzerman and Guy Lafleur each hit the 28-game mark. The closest rearguard is Paul Coffey, who scored an amazing 55 points during a 28-game stretch in 1985–86 with the offense-oriented Oilers. Bourque, no slouch either, ranks second with a 19-game streak and 27 points.

The NHL's Longest Point Streaks by Defensemen*

Player	Team	Season	Points	Games
Paul Coffey	Edmonton	1985–86	16–39–55	28
Ray Bourque	Boston	1987–88	6–21–27	19
Ray Bourque	Boston	1984–85	4–24–28	17
Brian Leetch	NYR	1991–92	5–24–29	17
Gary Suter	Calgary	1987–88	8–17–25	16
Bobby Orr	Boston	1970–71	10–23–33	15
Bobby Orr	Boston	1973–74	8–15–22	15
Steve Duchesne	Quebec	1992–93	4–17–21	15
Chris Chelios	Chicago	1995–96	4–16–20	15

*Current to 1997

3.3 **A. Eddie Shore**

Since its inception in 1924, the Hart Trophy has traditionally gone to the best offensive forwards of the game. Rarely has a defensemen been awarded league MVP honours. Even goalies have fared better than their defensive brethren in Hart voting—for example, Red Kelly's second-place finish to MVP-winning goalie Al Rollins, in 1954, and Doug Harvey's loss to goalie Jacques Plante, in 1962. Almost without exception, each generation of hockey writers has voted offense over defense and goalie over blueliner. Only Bobby Orr, who won three straight

Harts (1970, 1971, 1972), could sway the polls. Even then, Orr's MVP success was rooted in his prodigious point scoring. There have been two other D-men (Herb Gardiner in 1927 and Babe Pratt in 1944) who have claimed MVP awards, but it is Eddie Shore's four Harts between 1933 and 1938 that stand apart. Interestingly, although Shore wasn't a strong point-earner, he attracted more MVP votes than scoring champs Charlie Conacher and Bill Cook. Shore, like Orr, had a riveting on-ice presence, controlling games and turning them in his team's favour with his headlong rushes and puckhandling virtuosity. And he always played for keeps. Hard, fast hockey was Shore's game. He steamrolled opponents, and when they didn't go down he'd flatten them with his fists. A flying terror on the ice, Shore earned his MVPs as a character player with a heart the size of Boston Garden. He was the original Big Bad Bruin.

3.4 **C. 46 goals**
The NHL has always had a few great rushing defensemen. For D-men such as Eddie Shore, "Flash" Hollett and Doug Harvey, the position meant more than blocking shots, skating off attackers and staying back to defend their netminders. Unlike the majority of blueliners, they could take over on offense, move the puck and set up plays. Then came Bobby Orr. During his nine full NHL seasons between 1966 and 1975, Orr redefined the defenseman's role, revolutionizing the position with his electrifying, game-breaking brand of hockey. His puck-carrying and shooting skills were unlike those of any defenseman before him, and have since influenced a generation of Bourques, Leetches and Chelioses. Still, no defenseman but Orr has won a league scoring title. He twice accomplished the feat, including his 135-point season in 1974–75, the year of his highest goal output, 46 goals.

3.5 **B. 48 goals**
After Bobby Orr scored 46 goals in 1974–75, few figured another defenseman could top that mind-boggling num-

ber. Eleven years later, Paul Coffey smashed Orr's mark, tallying 48 goals in 1985–86. An extraordinarily gifted skater with the rushing and puckhandling skills of Orr, Coffey was perfectly suited to Edmonton's firewagon style of play. More than just a fast skater, Coffey's talent lay in his ability to make plays at lightning speed. While some criticized his defensive-end work, he finished the season with a +61 plus-minus rating. Yes, Coffey did surprise Orr's fans by outscoring the great Bruin, but they could take some comfort in knowing that Coffey finished 1985–86 with 138 points, one point less than Orr's NHL record of 139 points in 1970–71.

The NHL's Top Goal-Scoring Defensemen*

Player	Team	Season	Schedule	Goals
Paul Coffey	Edmonton	1985–86	80	48
Bobby Orr	Boston	1974–75	80	46
Paul Coffey	Edmonton	1983–84	80	40
Doug Wilson	Chicago	1981–82	80	39
Bobby Orr	Boston	1970–71	78	37
Bobby Orr	Boston	1971–72	78	37
Paul Coffey	Edmonton	1984–85	80	37
Kevin Hatcher	Washington	1992–93	84	34
Bobby Orr	Boston	1969–70	76	33
Bobby Orr	Boston	1973–74	78	32

*Current to 1997

3.6   D. 1944–45

Clancy. Cleghorn. Pratt. These old-time rearguards managed 14-, 17- and 18-goal seasons, but no D-man cracked the 20-goal barrier until 1944–45, when Detroit's Bill "Flash" Hollett scored 20 times in the 50-game schedule. Hollett played first in Toronto and later in Boston where he developed superb rushing and stickhandling skills under the guidance of Eddie Shore and Dit Clapper. In the stay-at-home era of blueliners, Hollett excelled in both setting up plays and goal production. He twice registered 19-goal seasons before his record-setting 20-goal performance in 1944–45. That season two NHL milestones were set: Hollett's 20-goal rearguard mark and Maurice Richard's 50-in-50 record (an achievement that overshadowed all other events). To put a modern spin on Hollett's feat, he was the only D-man in NHL history to post a 20-goal season before Bobby Orr scored 21 times in 1968–69. Hollett, as of 1997, had not been named to the Hockey Hall of Fame.

3.7 **C. Calgary's Al MacInnis**
No player in playoff annals has strung together a longer point-scoring streak than Bryan Trottier, who scored 29 points in 18 straight games in 1981. The next-best streak (17 games) is shared by Wayne Gretzky (1988) and defenseman Al MacInnis. With one of the game's hardest shots, MacInnis became a major factor in the Flames' Stanley Cup win in 1989. He led in playoff scoring with 31 points (7–24–31) and amassed a 17-game point-scoring streak on seven goals and 19 assists. It's the second-longest streak in playoff history and the longest among all D-men. MacInnis potted four game-winners, or one-fourth of Calgary's 16 victories. He was awarded the Conn Smythe Trophy as playoff MVP, only the fourth blueliner so honoured.

3.8 **C. Denis Potvin**
When Islanders general manager Bill Torrey drafted Potvin first overall in 1973, he was establishing the infrastructure for a team that would soon dominate the NHL. It didn't hurt that Torrey later drafted Clark Gillies, Bryan Trottier and Mike Bossy, but in Potvin he found the player to build his dynasty around. Potvin won the Calder Trophy as top rookie in 1973–74, scoring 54 points while manning the blueline. He soon became one of the game's most complete players: a run-and-gun threat on the rush, a quarterback on the power play and a punishing checker who left opponents groggy. After scoring 101 points in

Denis Potvin captained the New York Islanders to four Stanley Cups.

1978–79, Potvin captained New York to four straight championships, including a 25-point postseason in 1981's 18-game march to the Stanley Cup. When Potvin retired in 1988, he was the highest-scoring defenseman of all time, with 310 goals and 742 assists for 1,052 points.

3.9 D. Toronto's Ian Turnbull
Turnbull's hard shot, speed and natural ability made him one of the league's top defensemen in the 1970s. But his scoring touch could never compensate for his lackadaisical attitude and defensive lapses. Although his play was often uneven, when he wanted to he could turn it on. His best offensive night occured on February 2, 1977, against Detroit at Maple Leaf Gardens, when he banged home the NHL's only five-goal game by a blueliner.

3.10 A. Chicago's Pierre Pilote
One of the game's great rushers and thumpers, Pilote scored 59 points (14–45–59) in 1964–65's 70-game schedule, the rearguard record that Bobby Orr broke in 1968–69 with his 64-point effort. Who held the NHL scoring record for D-men before Pilote? The Chicago blueliner snapped Babe Pratt's 21-year-old mark of 57 points (17–40–57), set in the 50-game schedule of 1943–44.

3.11 A. Babe Pratt
Pratt was one of old-time hockey's best rushing rearguards. He could play the blueline (only 17 goals against with New York during their Stanley Cup-winning season in 1939–1940), but it was his offensive numbers that were unparalleled, especially during his record-setting 57-point season with Toronto in 1943–44. Pratt's best match came on January 8, 1944, when he recorded the NHL's first six-assist game by a defenseman (and only the second among all skaters) in a 12–3 Leaf win over Boston. His MVP-winning 57-point season stood for 21 years, but his six-assist game wasn't equalled until Chicago's Pat Stapleton did it in March 1969. Since then only four

REARGUARD GUNNERS: ANSWERS

other D-men, including Bobby Orr and Paul Coffey, have matched Pratt's assist mark.

3.12 C. Eight goals

One of the most unusual offensive marks established in one game is the record for most goals by two defensemen. Interestingly, the record wasn't set after, but before the great rearguard's (Bobby Orr's) hockey career: 40 years earlier on November 19, 1929. Between Toronto's Hap Day and Pittsburgh's Johnny McKinnon, the two defensemen scored eight times, four goals apiece, in the Pirates' 10–5 bombing over the Maple Leafs. The goal surge was likely due to the new offside and forward passing rules introduced at the start of 1929–30. Forward passing was legal in all three zones (there was no redline until 1943) and there were no illegal offsides except for passes from one zone to another. This caused a league-wide goal explosion that forced the NHL to rethink its new rules. Without precedent, the Day–McKinnon game must have had some impact. Less than a month after the game, one of the offside rules was amended, restricting attacking players from preceding the play when entering the opposing defensive zone.

3.13 B. 1969–70

Because the position is primarily defensive in nature, blueliners are rarely expected to be prolific goal scorers. But Bobby Orr altered that mindset with his historic first-place finish in 1969–70's scoring race. After scoring 41, 31 and 64 points between 1966 and 1969, Orr sent the hockey world reeling by firing 33 goals and 87 assists for 120 points, to become the first rearguard to win the Art Ross Trophy as the league's scoring champion. Orr's 33 goals established another milestone: the NHL's first 30-goal season by a blueliner. He was just 22 years old.

3.14 D. Five D-men

Orr, Coffey and Leetch are the easy, obvious choices. The other two? The Islanders' Denis Potvin and Calgary's Al

MacInnis. Orr, with six straight 100-point seasons, scored the fastest 100th point (1974–75) in just 57 games. Coffey had five 100-pointers between 1983–84 and 1989–90, Potvin had one in 1978–79, likewise for MacInnis in 1990–91 and Leetch in 1991–92.

3.15 C. Ray Bourque

Although a few goalies have been named both top rookie and a first team All-Star (including Tony Esposito in 1970 and Glenn Hall in 1956), no skater, until Ray Bourque, had ever won both honours in the same year. No one. Not even Bobby Orr, Gordie Howe or Mike Bossy ever achieved it. Bourque's first season, 1979–80, was a measure of his superb hockey instincts and a glimpse into the future. He won the Calder and his first All-Star team selection while setting an NHL record for rookie defensemen (65 points). Ever since, his offensive production, like his work ethic, has been tireless. Bourque has recorded nine 20-or-more-goal years, has led the Bruins in scoring five times, ranks second only to Gordie Howe with 17 straight All-Star selections, and has scored better than one point a game for 1,363 points through 1996–97. Like Doug Harvey and Bobby Orr before him, Bourque's awesome talent lies in his skating and shooting skills, his deep passion for hockey and his timing and anticipation, which allow him to orchestrate the pace of a game.

RETIRED NUMBERS

In this game, match the retired numbers below to the players who honoured them. Obviously, some of the same numbers have been retired by different teams. *(Solutions are on page 136)*

Jean Béliveau	Bill Barber	Sid Abel	Howie Morenz
Henri Richard	Stan Mikita	Bobby Orr	Denis Potvin
Phil Esposito	Rod Gilbert	Stan Smyl	Johnny Bucyk
Marcel Dionne	Doug Harvey	Bobby Hull	Bill Barilko
Gil Perreault	Ted Lindsay	Mike Bossy	Bobby Clarke
Lanny McDonald	Guy Lafleur	Brian Sutter	Alex Delvecchio
Maurice Richard	Dave Taylor	Eddie Shore	Michel Goulet

No. 2

_____

_____

No. 4

_____

_____

No. 5

_____

_____

No. 7

_____

_____

_____

No. 9

Gordie Howe

_____

_____

_____

No. 16

_____

_____

_____

No. 10

_____

_____

No. 11

_____

_____

No. 12

_____

_____

No. 18

_____

No. 21

_____

No. 22

_____

Chapter FOUR

THE GREAT ONE

No hockey player has inspired more quotes than Wayne Gretzky. They've come from journeymen, such as Bill Houlder, who said after his first shift against No. 99, "I didn't know whether to check him or ask for his autograph." And from Hall of Famers such as Gordie Howe, who concluded, "I sometimes think that if you part Wayne's hair, you'll find another eye." Scoring ace Marcel Dionne once said, "There's a record book for Wayne Gretzky and one for everyone else in the league." No argument here, considering Gretzky owns 61 NHL records and has collected more goals, assists and points than anyone else in history. So, here is the Wayne Gretzky chapter.

(Answers are on page 56)

4.1 **Against which team did Wayne Gretzky score his first professional goal?**
A. The Vancouver Canucks
B. The Edmonton Oilers
C. The Quebec Nordiques
D. The Indianapolis Racers

4.2 **What is the greatest number of games Wayne Gretzky has gone in his NHL career without scoring a goal?**
A. 12 games
B. 15 games
C. 18 games
D. 21 games

THE GREAT ONE: QUESTIONS

4.3 How many points did Wayne Gretzky score during his NHL record-setting, 51-game point-scoring streak in 1983–84?
A. Less than 100 points
B. Between 100 and 125 points
C. Between 125 and 150 points
D. More than 150 points

4.4 When did Wayne Gretzky register his NHL-record 92-goal season?
A. 1981–82
B. 1982–83
C. 1983–84
D. 1984–85

4.5 What is the greatest number of goals scored by Wayne Gretzky in the first 50 games from the start of a season?
A. 51 goals
B. 56 goals
C. 61 goals
D. 66 goals

4.6 Which team was Wayne Gretzky playing for when he counted his 100th playoff goal?
A. The Edmonton Oilers
B. The Los Angeles Kings
C. The St. Louis Blues
D. The New York Rangers

4.7 How many pages did the 1996–97 New York Rangers team guide devote to Wayne Gretzky?
A. Two pages
B. Four pages
C. Six pages
D. Eight pages

Wayne Gretzky. No. 99 rewrote the record book.

4.8 **What is the greatest number of goals scored by Wayne Gretzky during a season, including playoffs?**
   A. 92 goals
   B. 96 goals
   C. 100 goals
   D. 104 goals

THE GREAT ONE: QUESTIONS

4.9 In 1970–71, Phil Esposito fired an NHL high of 550 shots on net and scored a league record 76 goals. How many shots did Wayne Gretzky need in 1981–82 to break Espo's goal-scoring record?
A. 300 shots
B. 400 shots
C. 500 shots
D. 600 shots

4.10 How many shots on net did Wayne Gretzky take during his NHL-record, 92-goal season in 1981–82?
A. 319 shots
B. 369 shots
C. 419 shots
D. 469 shots

4.11 How many times did Wayne Gretzky break the 200-point plateau during his career?
A. Once
B. Twice
C. Three times
D. Four times

4.12 What historic goal did Wayne Gretzky score on December 21, 1991?
A. The goal that surpassed Maurice Richard's career total
B. The goal that surpassed Bobby Hull's career total
C. The goal that surpassed Phil Esposito's career total
D. The goal that surpassed Marcel Dionne's career total

4.13 In what year did/will Wayne Gretzky score his 3,000th combined regular-season and playoff point?
A. 1996–97
B. 1997–98
C. 1998–99
D. 1999–2000

Answers

THE GREAT ONE

4.1 B. The Edmonton Oilers
Before his NHL career began in 1979, Gretzky played the 1978–79 regular season split between the Indianapolis Racers (eight games) and the Edmonton Oilers (72 games) of the WHA. His first pro goal was anything but spectacular. It came on a weak fanned shot with the Racers—ironically, against the team he would later turn into an NHL dynasty, the Oilers. It happened on October 20, 1978, before 6,386 fans at Indianapolis' Market Place Arena. Gretzky scored another goal in the 4–3 loss, which history will record as his first multiple-goal game and his fourth pro start. Less than a year later, Gretzky scored his first NHL goal against the Vancouver Canucks on October 14, 1979.

4.2 D. 21 games
"The drought of '97," as it became known, turned into a goal-scoring dry spell without precedent in the 18-year history of hockey's greatest scorer. For 21 agonizing games (five games longer than his previous goal-less streak), from December 30, 1996, to February 21, 1997, the Great One wasn't so great. Although he had not stopped piling up assists to remain third in point totals, it was Gretzky's worst goal slump. "As time goes by, it wears on you," he said. You want to contribute more offensively." Tighter checking and Wayne's sore back were cited as contributing factors. Gretzky's own theory? "At the beginning of the year, I really concentrated on going to the net and if it opens up, making the play," he said. "Right now I'm trying to make the play and then go to

the net." The drought ended on a 50-foot shot at 17:54 of the second period in a 7–2 Rangers loss against Hartford. It was Gretzky's 17th of 1996–97, his 854th NHL career goal and the 900th goal of his professional career.

4.3 **D. More than 150 points**
Gretzky scored an astonishing 61 goals and 92 assists for 153 points during his record 51-game streak. It began on October 5, 1983, and continued uninterrupted for almost four months until Los Angeles Kings goaltender Markus Mattsson finally shut down No. 99 on January 28, 1984.

4.4 **A. 1981–82**
Gretzky smashed a number of hockey's most important scoring records in 1981–82, the season, as Gretzky says, "all heaven broke lose. Pucks just started going into the net on their own. I'd tip 'em in, bounce 'em in, wobble 'em in, elbow 'em in, wish 'em in. No matter what I tried, they kept finding their way past goaltenders." In one four-game stretch, Gretzky scored 10 goals. He nailed the 50-goal mark in just 39 games, broke Phil Esposito's 76-goal record and became the first player to score 200 points in a season. Teamed with Finnish sniper Jari Kurri, Gretzky was unstoppable. His brilliant 92-goal season set a new NHL standard. No hockey player has ever dominated a season like Gretzky did in 1981–82.

4.5 **C. 61 goals**
One of Gretzky's more obscure records is the league-high 61 goals he scored during Edmonton's first 50 games between October 8, 1981, and January 22, 1982. His 1.22 goals-per-game average levelled off in the final 30 games of the 80-game schedule, when he managed *only* a goal a game (for a total of 92 goals). Not unlike many of Gretzky's other records, in this category he tied himself for first place with another 61-goal rampage in 1983–84.

Most Goals in 50 Games from Start of Season*

Player	Team	Duration	Goals
Wayne Gretzky	Edm	10/07/81 to 1/22/82	61
Wayne Gretzky	Edm	10/05/83 to 1/25/84	61
Mario Lemieux	Pit	10/07/88 to 1/31/89	54
Wayne Gretzky	Edm	10/11/84 to 1/28/85	53
Brett Hull	StL	10/04/90 to 1/26/91	52
Maurice Richard	Mtl	10/28/44 to 3/18/45	50
Mike Bossy	NYI	10/11/80 to 1/24/81	50
Brett Hull	StL	10/05/91 to 1/28/92	50

*Current to 1997

4.6 **B. The Los Angeles Kings**

Gretzky became the first player in NHL history to score 100 playoff goals on May 7, 1993, during game three of the division finals against Vancouver. Although Gretzky reached the century mark first, his accomplishment was anything but assured going into the 1993 playoffs. Shadowing Gretzky, who had 95 playoff goals, was his teammate Jari Kurri, with 93 goals. Kurri notched his 100th playoff marker on May 21, just six games after Gretzky netted his 100th.

4.7 **D. Eight pages**

Every season, NHL clubs publish team guides, complete with regular-season and playoff records, franchise history and current player profiles. Each team member usually gets two pages devoted to his career. In some cases, exceptions are made. Players such as Mark Messier receive four pages because of their "star power" and contribution to hockey. On a higher level are Wayne Gretzky and Mario Lemieux, who each got eight pages in their teams' guides for 1996–97. Although both player profiles highlighted the usual year-by-year compendium of facts and stats, they differed in other respects. In the Rangers guide, three pages were devoted to Gretzky's NHL records; the Penguins guide used just a half-page for Lemieux's league records, but devoted a full page to his list of injuries. The Gretzky profile included a short bio on "The Legend of 99," while Lemieux's listed only a few interesting pieces of trivia. For example, which goalie has allowed the most goals by Lemieux? The answer: John Vanbiesbrouck.

4.8 **C. 100 goals**

As expected, the NHL mark for most goals in one regular season and postseason belongs to Wayne Gretzky. Perhaps not so well known is the fact that Gretzky didn't tally the league's best combined season during his record-breaking 92-goal regular season, 1981–82. That year, Gretzky scored five playoff goals in five games before his Edmonton Oilers were defeated by Los Angeles. No. 99's best goal-scoring year, including playoffs, came two years later in 1983–84, when he combined 87 regular-season goals and 13 playoff goals. Gretzky is the only player to crack the 100-goal plateau.

The NHL's Highest Goal Count (Regular and Postseason)*

Player	Team	Year	RS Goals	Playoff Goals	Total Goals
Wayne Gretzky	Edm	1983–84	87	13	100
Wayne Gretzky	Edm	1981–82	92	5	97
Mario Lemieux	Pit	1988–89	85	12	97
Brett Hull	StL	1990–91	86	11	97
Wayne Gretzky	Edm	1984–85	73	17	90
Jari Kurri	Edm	1984–85	71	19	90
Mike Bossy	NYI	1980–91	68	17	85
Brett Hull	StL	1989–90	72	13	85

*Current to 1997

4.9 A. 300 shots
Esposito scored 76 goals on 550 shots in 1970–71. Gretzky broke Espo's 11-year-old record on his 300th shot, firing goal number 77 of the season against Buffalo's Don Edwards on February 24, 1982.

4.10 B. 369 shots
To establish his NHL goal-scoring record of 92 goals in 1981–82, the Great One directed 369 shots on net in 80 games, an average of 4.6 shots per game, or, incredibly, a goal on every fourth shot on net.

4.11 D. Four times
Gretzky is the only NHLer to score 200 or more points in a season. Amazingly, he did it four times in five years while with Edmonton. The fifth season, 1982–83, he "stumbled" and recorded 196 points. The Great One scored 212 points in 1981–82; 205 points in 1983–84; 208 in 1984–85; and in his best season, 1985–86, 215 points, to set the NHL record. In five years Gretzky scored 1,036 points.

4.12 D. The goal that surpassed Marcel Dionne's career total
Gretzky's dominance on-ice and his influence off-ice is a large part of the story of North American hockey during the past two decades. With the possible exception of Michael Jordan, few athletes have influenced their respective sports like Gretzky. More than a superstar, Gretzky has become larger than the sport itself, a household name in a Canadian game largely unfamiliar to most Americans. Few, if any, have approached Gretzky's stature. He not only owns an astounding 61 NHL records, he championed the European invasion, playing alongside Finnish sniper Jari Kurri, and opened up the American Sunbelt markets to hockey. As the NHL's all-time scoring champion, Gretzky has surpassed the game's greatest scorers. On December 21, 1991, he notched his 732nd goal to pass Dionne, the last sniper in his path before his assault on Gordie Howe's 801-goal record.

THE GREAT ONE: ANSWERS

Wayne Gretzky's Milestone Goals

Career Goal No.	Date	Achievement
1	10/14/79	First NHL goal
50	04/02/80	First of eight straight 50-goal years
156	12/30/81	50 goals in 39 games
183	02/24/82	Scored 77th goal to break Phil Esposito's single-season record
198	03/26/82	Scored 92nd goal to set highest single-season total
325	01/18/84	Passed Nels Stewart's career goal total
500	11/22/86	Passed Mike Bossy's record for fastest 500 goals
545	10/14/87	Passed Maurice Richard's career goal total
611	12/23/88	Passed Bobby Hull's career goal total
641	10/15/89	Set all-time points total: 1,851
718	03/28/91	Passed Phil Esposito's career goal total
732	12/21/91	Passed Marcel Dionne's career goal total
802	03/23/94	Passed Gordie Howe's career goal total

4.13 **A. 1996–97**

Gretzky snared his milestone 3,000th point on a Luc Robitaille goal at 6:35 of the second period of a 6–2 Rangers win, against Montreal's Jocelyn Thibault, December 1, 1996. It was Gretzky's 1,473rd game, counting both regular-season and playoff contests. "I didn't even know it," Gretzky said. "Honest, I just saw it on TV."

Breakdown of Wayne Gretzky's 3,000th NHL Point

Games		Goals		Assists		Total Points	
Regular Season	Post-season	Regular Season	Post-season	Regular Season	Post-season	Regular Season	Post-season
1,280	193	846	112	1,792	250	2,638	362

Totals

1,473 games played: 958 goals + 2,042 assists = 3,000 points

Game FOUR

TEAM GOAL-LEADERS

In this game, we take a break from old-time trivia and offer you a modern-day challenge. Listed below are the first names of all 26 players who led their team in goal scoring during 1996–97. Once you've figured out their last names, find them in the puzzle by reading across, down or diagonally. Following our example of New Jersey's John M-A-C-L-E-A-N, connect the other 26 names (the Devils had a second goal leader in 1996–97), using letters no more than once. Start with the letters printed in heavy type.

(Solutions are on page 137)

Ray _____ Mats _____ John _____

Ray _____ Ted _____ Bill _____

Mike _____ Mark _____ Tony _____

Adam _____ Dino _____ Owen _____

Theo _____ Brett _____ Geoff _____

Teemu _____ Mark _____ Ryan _____

Mario _____ Keith _____ Peter _____

Alexi _____ Donald _____ Martin _____

Brendan _____ Zigmund _____

```
S R E D N A S U G
N O L O N I R E D O N
E D A S N A Y R U F A
A S N E M S O M E L T
D M Y L O H D A N O O
M A T H A N E P D R E
S R F E R N T P R C P
H Y A S H R N E A C A
  I M E L I A E H L
U E U S N R A I E M F
X N I N O U N-A L A F
S D D N D C E L C A Y
A R O E L U L L H M N
N A B T A H R A S E A
I L E T I E N S C C H
K U G K E R I E C I S
  H C A T I L L R A
```

Chapter FIVE

RECORD BREAKERS

Wayne Gretzky may hold the NHL's most important scoring records, but there are hundreds more that reveal other hockey stories. For example, there is the tale of scoring champ Joe Malone, who on a bitter January night in 1920, entered the NHL record books by notching the most goals in an NHL game. Because of the freezing temperatures, few witnessed Malone's historic game, but, 70 years later, he's still acknowledged as the record holder, which brings us to this chapter's first question. *(Answers are on page 67)*

5.1 What is the highest number of goals scored by one player in an NHL game?
  A. Five goals
  B. Six goals
  C. Seven goals
  D. Eight goals

5.2 What is the record for the longest consecutive goal-scoring streak in NHL history?
  A. 12 games
  B. 16 games
  C. 20 games
  D. 24 games

RECORD BREAKERS: QUESTIONS

5.3 **Among players with 20 goals or more in one season, what is the highest goals-per-game average in NHL history?**
A. 0.99 goals per game
B. 1.18 goals per game
C. 1.46 goals per game
D. 2.20 goals per game

5.4 **What is the fastest time from the start of an NHL game for a goal to be scored?**
A. Three seconds
B. Five seconds
C. Seven seconds
D. Nine seconds

5.5 **Who holds the record for the most penalty-shot goals?**
A. Steve Yzerman
B. Ted Kennedy
C. Mario Lemieux
D. Stan Mikita

5.6 **Who broke Maurice Richard's 544-goal career record?**
A. Montreal's Bernie Geoffrion
B. Chicago's Bobby Hull
C. Detroit's Gordie Howe
D. Boston's Phil Esposito

5.7 **Which sniper broke Nels Stewart's NHL career mark of 324 goals?**
A. Detroit's Gordie Howe
B. Montreal's Maurice Richard
C. Boston's Milt Schmidt
D. Detroit's Ted Lindsay

5.8 **What is the NHL record for the most shots on goal by one player in one season?**
A. 350 shots
B. 450 shots
C. 550 shots
D. 650 shots

THE GOAL SCORERS

5.9 What is the highest number of goals scored by an NHL team in one season?
A. Between 300 and 350 goals
B. Between 350 and 400 goals
C. Between 400 and 450 goals
D. More than 450 goals

5.10 What is the record for the most hat tricks (three-or-more-goal games) scored by one player in an NHL season?
A. Six hat tricks
B. 10 hat tricks
C. 12 hat tricks
D. 16 hat tricks

5.11 What is the fastest time from the start of a game that a game-winning goal has been scored?
A. At 0:07
B. At 1:07
C. At 2:07
D. At 4:07

5.12 Which star forward was almost sold for the record price of one million dollars during the early 1960s?
A. Montreal's Jean Béliveau
B. Chicago's Bobby Hull
C. Detroit's Alex Delvecchio
D. Toronto's Frank Mahovlich

5.13 Which Flyer scored the most goals during Philadelphia's NHL-record 35-game unbeaten streak in 1979–80?
A. Brian Propp
B. Bill Barber
C. Rick MacLeish
D. Reggie Leach

Answers

RECORD BREAKERS

5.1 **C. Seven goals**
In 100 years of NHL hockey, no more than 35 players have produced a five-goal game, and only seven players have notched six in a single game. Among those who have reached that lofty plateau, no player accomplished what Joe Malone of the Quebec Bulldogs did on January 31, 1920. Malone scored an astonishing seven goals against Ivan Mitchell in a 10–6 win against the Toronto St Pats. It was the fifth time (an NHL record) Malone racked up a five-or-more-goal game during his seven-year NHL career. Malone's favourite target was Ottawa's Clint Benedict, who was victimized three times in two five-goal games and one six-goal outburst. Malone also pumped in five against Toronto's Harry Holmes. It was Malone's relentless drive as a goal scorer, along with his slick stick work and skating, that earned him his status as the league's first big star. During the course of his Hall of Fame career, Malone scored 146 goals in 125 regular-season games.

5.2 **B. 16 games**
Despite all the old records that have been broken by today's snipers, no one has ever matched the 75-year-old NHL mark of the 16-game goal-scoring streak. (A few players have come close: Mario Lemieux netted 18 goals in a 12-game stretch in 1992–93, and the Kings' Charlie Simmer scored 17 goals in his 13-game run in 1979–80.) The unbreakable streak has stood since 1921–22, when Ottawa's Harry "Punch" Broadbent went on a 25-goal rampage in 16 straight games, from December 24, 1921, through February 15, 1922. Broadbent won the NHL scoring title that season with 32 goals in the 24-game schedule.

5.3   **D. 2.20 goals per game**

Not since the NHL's first season (1917–18) has anyone come close to Joe Malone's incredible record of 44 goals in 20 games for a 2.20 goals-per-game average. Although it's almost impossible to compare the two eras of hockey, the best mark among today's players is Wayne Gretzky's 1.18 average from 87 goals in 74 games in 1983–84. With apologies to past greats such as Cy Denneny, Newsy Lalonde and others with goal-a-game averages, below is a list of the modern era's best numbers.

The NHL's Modern-Day Goals-Per-Game Leaders*

Player	Team	Season	Games	Goals	Average
Wayne Gretzky	Edm	1983–84	74	87	1.18
Wayne Gretzky	Edm	1981–82	80	92	1.15
Mario Lemieux	Pit	1992–93	60	69	1.15
Mario Lemieux	Pit	1988–89	76	85	1.12
Brett Hull	StL	1990–91	78	86	1.10
Cam Neely	Bos	1993–94	49	50	1.02
Maurice Richard	Mtl	1944–45	50	50	1.00
Alex Mogilny	Buf	1992–93	77	76	.99
Mario Lemieux	Pit	1995–96	70	69	.99
Phil Esposito	Bos	1970–71	78	76	.97
Jari Kurri	Edm	1984–85	73	71	.97

*Current to 1997

5.4   **B. Five seconds**

Three players share the league record for the fastest goal from the start of a game. On December 20, 1981, Winnipeg's Doug Smail broke the five-year record of six seconds, when he streaked up the left side and blasted a 15-foot wrist shot past St. Louis' Paul Skidmore, a rookie making his NHL debut. Smail's goal came just five seconds after the opening face-off. The Islanders' Bryan Trottier (1984) and Alexander Mogilny of Buffalo (1991) have each since tied Smail's record.

Joe Malone. The NHL's first scoring champion.

Mario Lemieux. No one was any deadlier on a breakaway.

5.5 C. Mario Lemieux

Before Mario came along, the NHL was on a fairly consistent course regarding penalty-shot averages. Except for the record-high 29 shots called in 1934–35, the year the penalty-shot rule was introduced, many seasons averaged between five and 10 shots, the best years producing a high of 14 shots and six goals or a goalie success rate of about 58 per cent. Star players like Gordie Howe, Johnny Bucyk and Maurice Richard might hike the odds scoring two penalty-shot goals on two or three shots awarded during their long-term careers. Charlie Conacher netted the most goals on penalty shots, scoring three times on six attempts. Then in the 1980s and 1990s penalty shots skyrocketed, with 20 or more being awarded some seasons. But goalies prevailed, blocking more than shooters scored. The exception was Lemieux, who scored a league-record six penalty-shot goals on a record eight penalty shots, personally reversing the goalie average from 58 per cent to a mere 25 per cent. His six goals are three more than the next closest current penalty-shot scorers: Mats Sundin, Joe Mullen and Steve Yzerman.

5.6 **C. Detroit's Gordie Howe**
Almost 11 years to the day after Richard broke Nels Stewart's 324-goal career record with his 325th goal (November 8, 1952), Howe topped the Rocket's record of 544 goals with his goal number 545, November 10, 1963. Ironically, both Howe's record-tying 544th and record-breaking 545th came against Richard's former team, the Canadiens. Number 545 was a shorthanded goal against Charlie Hodge in a 3–0 Detroit victory. The shutout was the 94th of goalie Terry Sawchuk's career, a milestone that equalled the all-time mark established by George Hainsworth in 1937. Ironically, Hainsworth played most of his career with Montreal.

5.7 **B. Montreal's Maurice Richard**
The Rocket passed Stewart with career goal number 325 on November 8, 1952. The NHL record was broken before 14,563 rabid Forum fans who rocked the rafters after their hometown superstar streaked up-ice on a Butch Bouchard pass and rifled the puck past Chicago's Al Rollins. The standing ovation and puck presentation lasted 10 minutes. Afterwards, Stewart sent a telegram that read: "Congratulations on breaking record. Hope you will hold it for many seasons. Best of luck to you and rest of team." Richard remained the NHL's goal-scoring leader until his retirement in 1960. He ended his career with 544 goals.

5.8 C. 550 shots

As one hockey writer put it, "The NHL had never witnessed anything like the show put on by Boston's Phil Esposito in 1970–71." Espo established NHL records for goals (76) and points (152), as well as shots on net, an unreal 550 shots in the 78-game schedule.

5.9 C. Between 400 and 450 goals

Using coach Glen Sather's run-and-gun offense, the 1983–84 Edmonton Oilers pumped an NHL-record 446 goals past opposing netminders during an 80-game schedule. Wayne Gretzky led the offensive barrage, ringing up 87 goals, followed by Glenn Anderson's 54 red lights and Jari Kurri's 52. Defenseman Paul Coffey scored 40 times and Mark Messier 37. The watershed year produced another record high. So prolific were the Oilers in 1983–84 that even netminder Grant Fuhr had a great offensive season, compiling an NHL goalie record of 14 assists.

5.10 B. 10 hat tricks

Among his scoring records, Wayne Gretzky holds the mark for the most three-or-more-goal games in one season. In 1981–82, the Great One notched a record 10 hat tricks for Edmonton with six three-goal games, three four-goal games and one five-goal game. Mario Lemieux and Mike Bossy came close during their stellar careers. The pair tied for second spot with nine three-or-more-goal games in a season, but neither topped Gretzky, who amazingly pulled off another 10-hat-trick season two years later, in 1983–84. Those two seasons, 1981–82 and 1983–84, were Gretzky's highest goal-scoring years (92 and 87 goals).

5.11 A. At 0:07

Toronto's Charlie Conacher scored the fastest game-winner in league history on February 6, 1932. According to local press reports, "The near capacity crowd (in Toronto) had hardly settled in their seats when Charlie

Conacher opened the scoring. Handed the puck by Busher Jackson from the opening face-off, Conacher let loose a whistling drive from near the blueline that found the top corner of the net. Wilf Cude had little chance for the save." But Conacher's contribution to his record is only half the story in the 6–0 win. Leaf goalie Lorne Chabot stoned the Bruins through 60 minutes to help preserve Conacher's early game-winner—one of old-time hockey's least known pieces of trivia.

5.12 D. Toronto's Frank Mahovlich

During a party in 1962's All-Star break, Leaf co-owner Harold Ballard accepted a deal worth a record one million dollars from Chicago's Jack Norris in exchange for the services of Mahovlich. Norris knew that the Leafs were having trouble signing the Big M, and thought he had salted the deal after reportedly handing Ballard a $1,000 bill. But the next day sobering thoughts prevailed—not with the Blackhawks club but with the Maple Leafs. Toronto's board of directors refused to accept the transaction and the hastily delivered $1-million cheque from Chicago. It was a record amount for a player, but the Maple Leafs said no to the deal and Mahovlich was quickly signed to Toronto. That season Mahovlich led the Maple Leafs in scoring (36–37–73), as Toronto won both the regular-season title and the Stanley Cup.

5.13 D. Reggie Leach

The Flyers scored 154 goals and 240 assists for 394 points during their NHL-record 35-game unbeaten streak, October 14, 1979, to January 6, 1980. Philly's most prolific goal scorers were Leach (24–15–39), followed by Brian Propp (20–19–39), Bill Barber (20–17–37), Rick MacLeish (19–13–32), Ken Linseman (9–23–32), Paul Holmgren (9–9–18) and Bobby Clarke (6–28–34). The Flyers allowed 98 goals and played every NHL team (except Washington) during their 25–0–10 stretch. It is the longest undefeated streak of any team in the history of North American professional sports.

EVOLUTION OF A RECORD

When Wayne Gretzky passed Gordie Howe with his historic 802nd goal in 1994, he became the NHL's current career goal-scoring leader. But which player did Howe best to become the top goal producer? And who led the league as scoring champs before Gretzky and Howe? In this game, we trace the evolution of two NHL records: Part 1 covers career goal-leaders, Part 2 is on career point-leaders. Match the players and their corresponding record-breaking totals with the year they accomplished their feat. To make it interesting, we've added one name and one number that don't belong in either category. *(Solutions are on page 137)*

Part 1

Goal-Scoring Leaders

Gordie Howe	Phil Esposito	Joe Malone	Wayne Gretzky
Cy Denneny	Nels Stewart	Howie Morenz	Maurice Richard

Career Goals

146   246   270   301   324   544   801   863

Year	Career Goals	Scoring Leader
1919–20		
1922–23		
1933–34		
1936–37		
1951–52		
1962–63		
1993–94		

Part 2

Point-Scoring Leaders

Maurice Richard	Syd Howe	Cy Denneny	Nels Stewart
Stan Mikita	Bill Cowley	Elmer Lach	Gordie Howe
Joe Malone	Howie Morenz	Wayne Gretzky	

Career Points

100   315   467   515   528   548   610   946
1,850   2,135   2,705

Year	Career Points	Point Leaders
1919–20	_____	_____
1928–29	_____	_____
1931–32	_____	_____
1938–39	_____	_____
1944–45	_____	_____
1946–47	_____	_____
1951–52	_____	_____
1953–54	_____	_____
1959–60	_____	_____
1988–89	_____	_____

Chapter SIX

THE BIG LINES

At one time, it seemed as though every team had its Big Line—a trio of forwards who combined breathtaking speed with gritty play and awesome scoring power. This three-way chemistry propelled what were otherwise ordinary teams to championships. These lethal combos were game-winners and dynasty builders. Whatever happened to hockey's great scoring lines? In this chapter, we look at the lines that could hurt you on every shift. *(Answers are on page 81)*

6.1 How many goals did the New York Rangers' GAG Line (Goal-a-Game) score during its peak season, the 78-game schedule of 1971–72?
A. 78 goals
B. Between 79 and 99 goals
C. Between 100 and 129 goals
D. More than 129 goals

6.2 Which left-winger played the longest on the Edmonton Oilers' Wayne Gretzky–Jari Kurri Line?
A. Craig Simpson
B. Esa Tikkanen
C. Mike Krushelnski
D. Pat Hughes

THE BIG LINES: QUESTIONS

6.3 **What was the name of Stan Mikita's famous line in Chicago?**
A. The Scooter Line
B. The Pony Line
C. The Reject Line
D. The Million-Dollar Line

6.4 **Who formed Toronto's most famous scoring trio, The Kid Line?**
A. Frank Selke
B. Charlie Conacher
C. Conn Smythe
D. King Clancy

6.5 **What entire line was traded away by Toronto in 1947?**
A. The Maple Leaf Line
B. The Kid Line
C. The Blue Line
D. The Flying Forts Line

6.6 **Who were "The Gold Dust Twins?"**
A. Chicago's Bobby Hull and Stan Mikita
B. Montreal's Odie and Sprague Cleghorn
C. The Rangers' Bill and Bun Cook
D. Ottawa's Cy Denneny and Punch Broadbent

6.7 **What 1970s team had its most famous line named after an Academy Award-winning movie?**
A. The New York Rangers
B. The Buffalo Sabres
C. The Los Angeles Kings
D. The Minnesota North Stars

6.8 **The Boston Bruins' line of Wayne Cashman, Phil Esposito and Ken Hodge was given what nickname?**
A. The Bonanza Line
B. The Nitro Line
C. The Grande Trio
D. The Bee Line

6.9 **Which prominent New York scoring unit is pictured above?**
   A. The Dynamite Line
   B. The Broadway Line
   C. The Cook–Boucher–Cook Line
   D. The Colville–Shibicky–Colville Line

6.10 **Which three NHLers formed the famed S Line?**
   A. The Maroons' Nels Stewart, Babe Siebert and Hooley Smith
   B. The Bruins' Derek Sanderson, Al Sims and Fred Stanfield
   C. The Hawks' Glen Skov, Tod Sloan and George Sullivan
   D. The Rangers' Alex Shibicky, Clint Smith and Earl Seibert

6.11 **The players on which line finished the 1949–50 season ranked first, second and third in the NHL scoring race?**
A. Detroit's Production Line
B. Montreal's Punch Line
C. Boston's Kraut Line
D. Chicago's Pony Line

6.12 **What is the highest point total produced by the Los Angeles Kings' Triple Crown Line in one season?**
A. 252 points
B. 302 points
C. 352 points
D. 402 points

6.13 **From which Canadian town did all the members of Boston's legendary Kraut Line come from?**
A. Brandon, Manitoba
B. Granby, Quebec
C. Weyburn, Saskatchewan
D. Kitchener, Ontario

6.14 **What country did the KLM Line play for in international hockey competition?**
A. The USA
B. Sweden
C. The Soviet Union
D. Holland

6.15 **Over its lifetime, how many Canadien forwards played *regularly* on Montreal's Doughnut Line?**
A. One forward: John Ferguson, the team's policeman
B. Two forwards: Guy Lafleur and Steve Shutt
C. Two forwards: Jean Béliveau and Henri Richard
D. Three forwards: Maurice Richard, Elmer Lach and Toe Blake

6.16 **Which two wingers did Bryan Trottier centre on the New York Islanders' Long Island Lighting Co.?**
A. Clark Gillies and Mike Bossy
B. John Tonelli and Bob Nystrom
C. Duane Sutter and Brent Sutter
D. Butch Goring and Bill Harris

6.17 **How many Stanley Cups did the Montreal Canadiens' famous Punch Line win as a scoring unit?**
A. Two Stanley Cups
B. Four Stanley Cups
C. Six Stanley Cups
D. Eight Stanley Cups

Answers

THE BIG LINES

6.1 **D. More than 129 goals**
Vic Hadfield, Jean Ratelle and Rod Gilbert played together on the New York Rangers' GAG Line for more than a decade—from the early 1960s to the mid-1970s. Even though they never won a Stanley Cup, at least longevity was on their side. It proved an important factor during their best season, 1971–72, when they produced 139 goals in the 78-game schedule. Only Phil Esposito and Bobby Orr's spectacular one-two finish topped the GAG Line's surprising third-, fourth- and fifth-place ranking in the NHL scoring derby—a race that included such snipers as Bobby Hull, Frank Mahovlich and Yvan Cournoyer. Bolstered by the GAG Line's scoring production, the Rangers reached the Cup finals that year, only to lose in six games to Bobby Orr's Bruins.

6.2 **B. Esa Tikkanen**
With the exception of Philadelphia's Legion of Doom Line, few teams in the 1980s and 1990s have found the right player combination to form a potent threesome. Two-man units with a third forward in rotation has become the norm. It's not because of any particular hockey philosophy, but today there are more teams, less depth of talent, and fewer coaches willing to let lines develop as pressure mounts for instant success. When Gretzky and Kurri teamed up in the early 1980s, their mobility and tremendous offensive skills became the vanguard for the Oilers' flying assault. Kurri could switch lanes in mid-attack to feed Gretzky. Gretzky, from any angle, but especially from behind the opponent's net, would set up Kurri for a one-timer or score himself on the wraparound. They knew each other's positions on the

ice almost without looking. Playing together became second nature. Many left-wingers guested on the line; the most frequent was Tikkanen, who played with the duo for almost three full seasons, winning two Stanley Cups and racking up phenomenal numbers. In 1986–87, the trio combined for 369 points.

6.3 **A. The Scooter Line**
The Blackhawks have a rich history of monikers for their scoring lines. Bobby Hull, Bill Hay and Murray Balfour were temporarily called the Scooter Line before they officially became the Million-Dollar Line; the 1940's Pony Line joined Bill Mosienko and brothers Doug and Max Bentley; the early 1990's Reject Line teamed fourth-liners Greg Gilbert, Christian Ruuttu and Dirk Graham. However, Chicago's real Scooter Line was powered by Doug Mohns, Stan Mikita and Kenny Wharram, a trio of speedsters, who, in 1964–65, accounted for almost half of Chicago's goals.

6.4 **C. Conn Smythe**
Smythe's rebuilding job of the Leafs in the late 1920s began in earnest with the signing of youngster Joe Primeau in 1927. Others were contracted, but before long Primeau was back in the minors for a year of seasoning. Then, in 1929, Smythe brought up a couple of kids, Busher Jackson and Charlie Conacher, from Frank Selke's old junior team, the Toronto Marlboros. On December 29, 1929, Smythe sent Jackson and Conacher out on a line with the struggling Primeau. It was pure magic. Chemistry on ice. They became the Kid Line and quickly developed into a trio of fearless young bloods characterized by their on-ice flair, bravado and scoring skill. In 1931–32, the threesome finished first (Jackson—53 points), second (Primeau—50) and fourth (Conacher—48) in the scoring race and helped Toronto win its first Stanley Cup under the Maple Leaf banner. Smythe had built his Cup winner and, in the process, one of hockey's most enduring skating and scoring legacies, the Kid Line.

THE BIG LINES: ANSWERS

6.5 **D. The Flying Forts Line**
Despite winning the Stanley Cup in 1947, Leaf general manager Conn Smythe knew he needed additional strength down the centre to complement the work of centremen Syl Apps and Ted Kennedy. Smythe found his man in Chicago: defending scoring champion Max Bentley. To get him (and unknown Cy Thomas), Smythe gave up his highly touted and talented Flying Forts Line of Gus Bodnar, Bud Poile and Gaye Stewart, as well as defensemen Bob Goldham and Ernie Dickens. Smythe pulled off the biggest trade to date, and it worked like magic. Toronto won three more Cups in four years with Bentley. Chicago, despite its new personnel, failed to make the playoffs for six seasons. By that time, only Bodnar from the Flying Forts Line remained. How did the line get its name? All three linemates were from Fort William, Ontario.

6.6 **D. Ottawa's Cy Denneny and Punch Broadbent**
During the 1920s, the old Ottawa Senators were *the* team to be reckoned with in the NHL. They finished in first place six times and won four Stanley Cups. Three of those championships came on the backbone of linemate wingers Denneny and Broadbent, who were called the Gold Dust Twins for their sparkling and gritty playing style. Acting as both policemen and triggermen, they kept the opposition honest while providing a potent offensive combination. In 1921–22's 24-game schedule, the Twins finished one-two in the NHL scoring race, Broadbent leading with a 32–14–46 record to Denneny's 27–12–39. In the 1923 best-of-three final series against Edmonton, Denneny and Broadbent each scored game-winners to claim the Stanley Cup. The pair was split up in 1924, when Broadbent moved to the Montreal Maroons.

6.7 **B. The Buffalo Sabres**
The hit movie *The French Connection* was the inspiration for Buffalo's greatest scoring unit of Rick Martin, Gilbert Perreault and Rene Robert. All native Quebecers, the trio

played together for eight years and in its most productive season, 1974–75, combined for 131 goals. During the playoffs, the French Connection Line was the driving force behind the Sabres' run to the Stanley Cup finals. The name was created by Buffalo reporter Lee Coppola, who got imaginative one night while operating Buffalo Auditorium's scoreboard.

6.8 **B. The Nitro Line**

The Nitro Line came together in the late 1960s after Phil Esposito was traded to Boston from Chicago. With the Blackhawks, Espo was Bobby Hull's centre and considered a caddy for the All-Star left-winger. But in Boston, Esposito hit paydirt with Cashman and Hodge. They worked the corners while Espo parked himself in the slot. Immovable, his sheer strength kept him in position for loose pucks. Espo was called the ultimate garbageman. His response? "They don't ask how, they ask 'How many?'" Cashman, Esposito and Hodge played together for more than five seasons on the Nitro Line in Boston, where in 1970–71 they exploded for 140 goals, 35 per cent of the Bruins' total offensive production. That was just the start. Esposito won four straight scoring titles and, in 1973–74, the unit iced their best season: 148 goals. Between Bobby Orr and the threesome, the Bruins swept the top four positions in the scoring race that year. Boston finished with a 52–17–9 record on the strength of its NHL record-setting 349 goals. Most important, Boston won two championships during that era. Curiously, in neither of the Nitro Line's two top seasons, 1970–71 and 1973–74, did the Bruins win the Cup.

6.9 **C. The Cook–Boucher–Cook Line**

When the New York Rangers joined the NHL in 1926, they obtained three players from the disbanded Western Hockey League—centre Frank Boucher, and brother wingers Bill and Bun Cook—who gave the club instant credibility. In their first season, the expansion Rangers, under Lester Patrick, finished atop the American Division;

Bill Cook won the scoring NHL title (33-4-37). The next season, the Rangers claimed the Stanley Cup, turning New Yorkers into lifelong hockey fans. As Frank Boucher explained in Stan Fischler's *20th Century Hockey Chronicle*, he and the Cook brothers clicked as a line from the start. "We never put diagrams on paper. Somehow, just in describing our ideas, we'd all grasp it. Bill would do most of the talking. He'd say, 'Now look, when I want that puck I'll yell for it, and you get that damn puck to me when I yell. Don't look up to see where I am; just put it there and I'll be there.'" One of their most innovative plays was the drop pass, a ploy they worked to perfection. The Cook–Boucher–Cook Line (aka the Bread Line) played together for 10 years, and won another Cup for New York in 1933.

6.10 A. The Maroons' Nels Stewart, Babe Siebert and Hooley Smith

The S Line of Stewart, Siebert and Smith was formed in the late 1920s and played together for five seasons with the Montreal Maroons. Stewart centred the line and was its leading point earner, but the unit's real strength was its combination of scoring power and tough play. Running roughshod over opponents, the S Line usually topped 200 minutes in box time, a high penalty count for a scoring line in that era. They became hockey's most feared threesome: Stewart, the gifted goal scorer; Siebert, the fierce competitor with great athletic strength; and Smith, with his sweeping hook-check, one of the game's best two-way players. As powerful and punishing as they were together, the line was broken up by two sudden trades in 1932. Stewart went to the Bruins and Siebert to the Rangers. Unlike most other scoring trios, their best years were not behind them after they split up. Stewart would win the NHL scoring crown again in 1937, Smith captained the Maroons to a Stanley Cup in 1935 and Siebert developed into an MVP-winning defenseman and Cup winner with the Rangers and Canadiens. All three S Line members are in the Hockey Hall of Fame.

6.11 **A. Detroit's Production Line**
Perhaps hockey's greatest trio, the fabled Production Line of Gordie Howe, Sid Abel and Ted Lindsay finished first-second-third in 1949–50's scoring race with Lindsay's record of 23–55–78, Abel's 34–35–69 and Howe's 35–33–68. It was not the first time three linemates had led the NHL in scoring, but it gave notice of Detroit's future dominance as an NHL powerhouse. The Red Wings won seven straight regular-season championships and four Stanley Cups (in five years) with the Production Line motoring their offense. Like other formidable scoring lines, the Production Line had great

Detroit's Production Line was powered by Gordie Howe, Sid Abel and Ted Lindsay.

chemistry. Abel was the unit's veteran, the savvy leader who centred the younger Lindsay and Howe. The pair blended superb skills and bone-jarring toughness—a lethal combination. Both men won NHL goal-scoring titles and often ranked among the league leaders in penalty minutes. Howe, on right wing, could do everything. His enormous strength and coordination made him a scoring champion for four straight years while playing with Lindsay and Abel (and later Alex Delvecchio). The Production Line played together for almost six years before Abel moved to Chicago as a player-coach.

6.12 **C. 352 points**

The Kings' Triple Crown Line possessed everything required of an elite scoring unit. In Marcel Dionne, the line had the consummate goal scorer and puck-carrying centre. Dave Taylor was the hulking cornerman and an excellent puck handler. Charlie Simmer, the finisher, was immovable in the crease while waiting for rebounds and tip-ins. More than individual speed, skill or strength, the trio meshed because all three players shared good communication—the ability to read off each other. In six seasons together, they averaged 284 points per year. Their best year was 1980–81, when each recorded more than 100 points: Dionne scoring 58 goals and 135 points, Taylor, 47 goals and 112 points and Simmer, 56 goals and 105 points.

6.13 **D. Kitchener, Ontario**

The Bruins' potent scoring line of Milt Schmidt, Woody Dumart and Bobby Bauer was formed in 1937–38, and almost immediately became known as the Kraut Line, a reference to the trio's Germanic hometown—Kitchener, in southern Ontario. (The small community was mostly settled by German immigrants in the 1800s.) In their first season, the wide-eyed kids from Kitchener combined for 46 goals and 88 points, not enough for a top 10 finish among them, but it was obvious that Schmidt, Dumart and Bauer read one another very well. The following season Boston won the Stanley Cup and the year after that, the Kraut Line paced the league one-two-three in scoring. Boston took another Cup in 1941, before the entire Kraut Line joined the Royal Canadian Air Force to play for the Allan Cup-winning Ottawa Hurricanes during World War II. Their NHL return three years later showed that the trio had lost none of its playmaking chemistry. They never won another Cup together, but each maintained his scoring drive. Bauer retired in 1946–47 after a career-high 30-goal season. Dumart and Schmidt played on until the mid-1950s. Dumart recorded five 20-goal years and three All-Star berths. Schmidt won the Hart

Trophy as league MVP in 1951. The Kraut Line's final game was on March 18, 1952. Bauer came out of retirement to play with his hometown teammates one more time at a game honouring Schmidt and Dumart. That night, Boston fans saw again what three boys from a small Canadian town could do together on ice, as Schmidt scored his landmark 200th career goal.

6.14 **C. The Soviet Union**
The famed unit of Vladimir Krutov, Igor Larionov and Sergei Makarov dominated Russian and international hockey for eight years during the 1980s, winning four world championships (1982, 1983, 1986, 1989) and two Olympic gold medals (in 1984 in Sarajevo and in 1988 in Calgary). The Krutov–Larionov–Makarov troika powered the Central Red Army Team to eight straight Soviet League titles. Makarov was named "Soviet Player of the Year" three times, Larionov once, and Krutov won the Gold Stick in 1986–87 as the outstanding player in Europe. When Soviet emigration restrictions eased, a number of players joined the NHL ranks in 1989, including Larionov and Krutov, who went to Vancouver, and Makarov, who went to Calgary. Krutov, considered the best pro prospect, was a bust after one season. Makarov, at 31, won the Calder Trophy as rookie of the year in 1990 and played six NHL seasons with Calgary and San Jose. Larionov, after stints in Vancouver and San Jose, centred Scotty Bowman's five-man Russian unit in Detroit.

6.15 **B. Two forwards: Guy Lafleur and Steve Shutt**
Canadiens defenseman Pierre Bouchard nicknamed Lafleur and Shutt's 1970s scoring line the Doughnut Line, because the two wingers played with "a hole in the centre," first filled by Henri Richard, then Pete Mahovlich and, finally, Jacques Lemaire. None of the three centres lasted more than two years with the Lafleur-Shutt duo, but over seven seasons the centres were instrumental in five Canadiens' Stanley Cups.

Except for Mahovlich, no Doughnut Line members were very big, but they were all great puck handlers and skaters. "Lafleur had to control the puck, I could dart to the holes and Lemaire could read the play from behind," Shutt once said.

6.16 A. Clark Gillies and Mike Bossy

Some great lines just happen, others are designed by general managers and coaches for success. For the Long Island Lighting Co. (aka the Grande Trio), it was "intuition" according to ex-Islanders general manager Bill Torrey, who drafted Trottier and Gillies in 1974 and Bossy in 1977. Bossy, the gifted junior from Quebec, had trouble finding his place on the roster until he was teamed with rising stars Gillies and Trottier. They first clicked halfway through their first game together, on an unforgettable play. "It was like tic-tac-toe," Torrey recalls, "and then the puck was in the net." The unit gelled, then went on to score 134 goals in 1977–78, including Bossy's league rookie-record of 53. The Long Island Lighting Co. was together nine seasons and helped the Islanders win four Stanley Cups between 1980 and 1983.

6.17 A. Two Stanley Cups

Despite its fame, the Punch Line of Toe Blake, Elmer Lach and Maurice Richard won only two Stanley Cups (1944 and 1946) for Montreal. Coach Dick Irvin, Sr., formed the trio in Richard's first full season, 1943–44. It was Lach's fourth season and Blake's 10th. Their age disparity (Blake was Richard's senior by nine years) had little effect on the unit's chemistry, but it did impact on its longevity. The Punch Line played together less than five seasons, but, in that short time, it revitalized the Canadiens franchise, ending a 13-year championship drought with the 1944 Cup win. Each full season the Punch Line played together, Montreal finished first overall. But perhaps the line's greatest contribution to the game, and that which it is most revered for, is Richard's 50-goals-in-50-games record—still the measuring stick for goal scorers. The line's last game was on January 8, 1948. Blake's career ended that night, when he broke his ankle after being heavily checked into the boards by Ranger defenseman Bill Judza.

Game Six

THE PINWHEEL PUZZLE

In this pinwheel puzzle, each word joins in the same way as a regular crossword. Starting at square No. 1, work clockwise around the four concentric rings or towards the centre along the spokes, filling in the right answer from the clues below. Each answer begins with the last letter of the previous word. Determine word length by using the clue numbers. For example, the answer to No. 3 is five letters long since the next clue is No. 5 from the list below.

(Solutions are on page 138)

Towards Centre
1. Wayne _____
2. Inspire
4. 1990s Devils No. 15, John _____
6. 1940–50s Canadiens, Maurice _____
8. 1970s Ranger, Jean _____
10. 1990s Tampa No. 19, Brian _____
11. Arena (4 letters),
12. 1990s Whalers No. 18, Robert _____
13. 1940s famous Leaf, Bill _____
15. Scoring _____
18. 1970s Flyer D-man, Ed _____
20. 1990s Oiler No. 29, Louie _____
21. Taken out of the play

Around
3. 1990s Tampa No. 85, Petr _____
5. 1980s Oiler, Glenn _____
7. 1960s Red Wing, Norm _____
9. 1970–80s Bruin, Peter _____
10. 1970s Hawk centre, Ivan _____
12. 1997 Dallas sniper, Pat _____
14. 1980s Flyer sniper, Tim _____
16. 1970s Ranger, _____ Gilbert
17. New Jersey player
19. Be ahead
20. Detroit ironman, Alex _____
22. 1980–90s Wing–Ranger, John _____

23. 1960–70s Leaf, Ron _____
24. Avalanche captain, Joe _____
25. Let go from team
26. 1980–90s Flyer-Pen, Rick _____
27. Franchise
28. 1990s Leaf, _____ Sundin
29. Finnish sniper, Tomas _____
30. 1980s Jet, Paul _____
31. 1980–90s Star-Devil No. 7
32. Modano's jersey number
33. _____ Muller
34. _____ the pressure on
35. _____ Bure
36. 1970s Canadien, Guy _____
37. 1970s Habs coach, Claude _____
38. _____ Robitaille
39. _____ of the crop
40. Bad crowd
41. 1960–70s Bruin, Johnny _____
42. 1980s Bruin, Gord _____
43. 1990s D-man, _____ Racine
44. Underhanded
45. Camille Henry nickname
46. 1940s Leaf D-man, Vic _____
47. Devils' state, (abbr.)
48. Teams lose, coaches lose their _____
49. Captains _____ for the team
50. 1940s Leaf trio, The _____ Line
51. 1920–30s Leaf, Hap _____

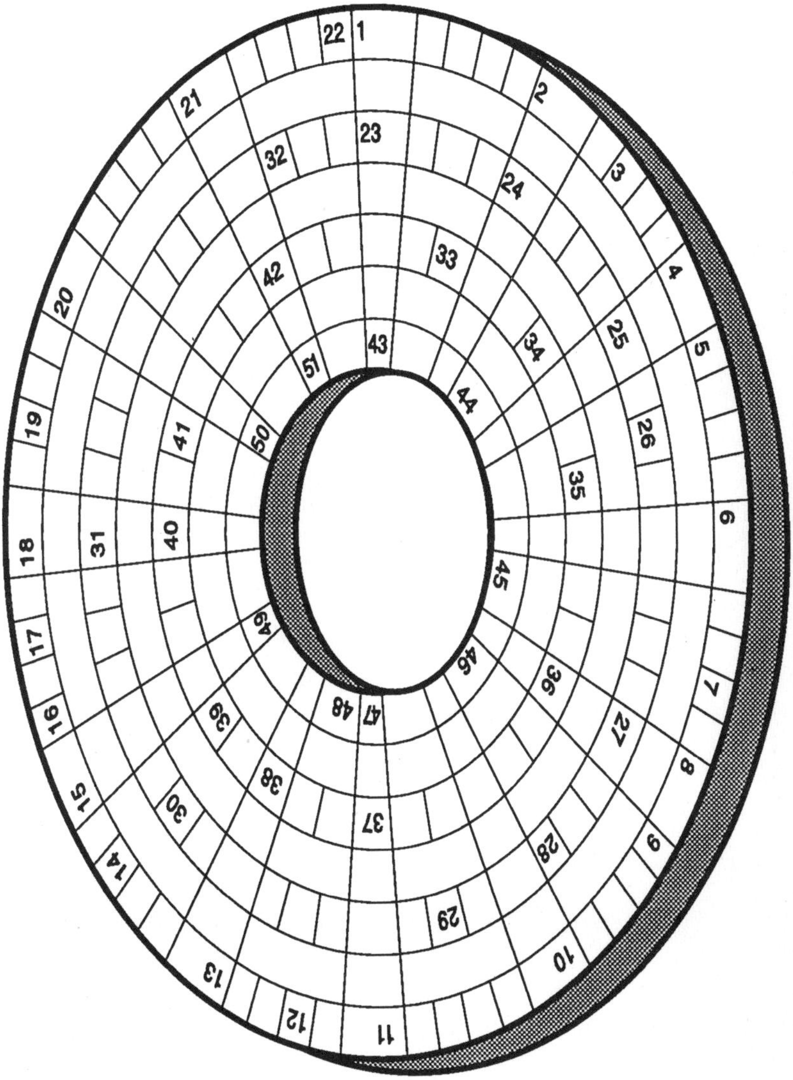
1
2
3
4
5
6
7
8
9
10
11
12
13
14
15
16
17
18
19
20
21
22
23
24
25
26
27
28
29
30
31
32
33
34
35
36
37
38
39
40
41
42
43
44
45
46
47
48
49
50
51

Chapter SEVEN

MILESTONES

Records are meant to be broken. But milestones? They live on as equity, enshrining a player's reputation long after his career ends. When Maurice Richard recorded hockey's first 50-goal season in 1944–45, it was the most remarkable achievement to date. In those days of woollen sweaters, barefaced goalies and five-digit wages, no one imagined it possible. The 50-goal season—today, it is still the goal scorer's most important standard. *(Answers are on page 99)*

7.1 **Considering the NHL began in 1917–18, in which season did the league produce its first 300-goal scorer? (And who was he?)**
 A. 1928–29
 B. 1938–39
 C. 1948–49
 D. 1958–59

7.2 **Which NHLer was the first to reach 500 career goals?**
 A. Nels Stewart
 B. Gordie Howe
 C. Maurice Richard
 D. Bobby Hull

Phil Esposito was a five-time NHL scoring champion.

7.3 **Which of the following players scored his 500th goal first?**
A. Bobby Hull
B. Frank Mahovlich
C. Jean Béliveau
D. Phil Esposito

7.4 **How many American-born players have scored 500 goals in the NHL?**
A. None
B. One player
C. Two players
D. Three players

7.5 **Against which goalie did Gordie Howe score both his milestone 500th and 600th goals?**
A. Glenn Hall
B. Terry Sawchuk
C. Gump Worsley
D. Johnny Bower

THE GOAL SCORERS

7.6 Which 500-goal scorer required the most games to reach that historic milestone?
A. Stan Mikita
B. Johnny Bucyk
C. Mark Messier
D. Lanny McDonald

7.7 How old was Gordie Howe when he scored his 100-point NHL season?
A. Less than 30 years old
B. Between 30 and 35 years old
C. Between 35 and 40 years old
D. More than 40 years old

7.8 Who was the first NHLer to score 100 points in a season?
A. Gordie Howe
B. Bobby Hull
C. Stan Mikita
D. Phil Esposito

7.9 When Phil Esposito became the NHL's first 100-point player, he scored point number 100 in his 60th game of 1968–69. The NHL's second 100-point man was Bobby Hull. How many more games did it take Hull to reach his 100th point in that same season?
A. One game more
B. Three games more
C. Seven games more
D. 11 games more

7.10 Who was the first 50-goal scorer to record 100 penalty minutes in the same season?
A. Bernie Geoffrion
B. Vic Hadfield
C. Johnny Bucyk
D. Jean Pronovost

MILESTONES: QUESTIONS

7.11 **After Wayne Gretzky, who is the youngest player to score 50 goals?**
A. Jimmy Carson
B. Paul Kariya
C. Pierre Larouche
D. Bobby Hull

7.12 **Who shares the record with Wayne Gretzky for the most 50-goal seasons?**
A. Bobby Hull
B. Guy Lafleur
C. Phil Esposito
D. Mike Bossy

7.13 **Among the 26 500-goal scorers (to 1997), how many have never recorded a 50-goal season in their careers?**
A. None; every 500-goal scorer had a 50-goal season
B. One player
C. Three players
D. Five players

7.14 **How many NHLers have scored 50 goals in *less* than 50 games? Name them, too.**
A. Three players
B. Four players
C. Five players
D. Six players

7.15 **The NHL's fastest 100 goals (from the start of a career) were scored in how many games?**
A. Less than 120 games
B. Between 120 and 140 games
C. Between 140 and 160 games
D. More than 160 games

7.16 **What does hockey's legendary number 544 represent?**
A. Maurice Richard's career goal-scoring total
B. Phil Esposito's NHL record for most shots on goal
C. Wayne Gretzky's career playoff-point total
D. Dave Schultz's NHL record for most penalty minutes

7.17 In his 32-year pro career, for how many consecutive seasons did Gordie Howe score 20 or more goals?
A. 11 consecutive seasons
B. 16 consecutive seasons
C. 21 consecutive seasons
D. 27 consecutive seasons

7.18 How many games did it take Bobby Hull and Brett Hull to each score their 500th goals?
A. Bobby: 771 games, Brett: 603 games
B. Bobby: 801 games, Brett: 633 games
C. Bobby: 831 games, Brett: 663 games
D. Bobby: 861 games, Brett: 693 games

7.19 How many more games did Mario Lemieux take to score 600 goals than Wayne Gretzky?
A. Lemieux scored his 600th faster than Gretzky
B. One game
C. Seven games
D. 17 games

7.20 In what chronological order did Wayne Gretzky, Phil Esposito, Marcel Dionne and Gordie Howe score their 700th goals?
A. 1) Howe, 2) Esposito, 3) Gretzky, 4) Dionne
B. 1) Howe, 2) Dionne, 3) Esposito, 4) Gretzky
C. 1) Esposito, 2) Howe, 3) Dionne, 4) Gretzky
D. 1) Howe, 2) Esposito, 3) Dionne, 4) Gretzky

7.21 Who is the youngest NHLer to score 1,000 points, besides Wayne Gretzky and Mario Lemieux?
A. Mike Bossy
B. Guy Lafleur
C. Steve Yzerman
D. Dale Hawerchuk

Answers

MILESTONES

7.1 **B. 1938–39**

The NHL's first 300-goal scorer was Nels Stewart, a hulking centre who played 15 years with the Montreal Maroons, Boston Bruins and New York Americans. Although Stewart, at six foot one, 195 pounds, equalled the average height and weight of today's player, he towered above the rest of the league in his era. He may not have been as nimble-footed as other forwards, but he used his size to shoot fast and play tough, something that became evident during his first season. As rookie starts go, Stewart's was nothing short of incredible. The Maroons freshman won the 1925–26 scoring title (42 points), took home the Hart Trophy as MVP and scored six of Montreal's 10 playoff goals to lead the second-year Maroons to the Stanley Cup. At the same time, he amassed 119 minutes in box time, an extraordinary penalty record for a forward. Few could stop him. In 1930, Stewart was teamed with Hooley Smith and Babe Siebert to form the Maroons' dreaded S Line. He collected a career-high 55 points, won the Hart again and scored 39 goals in 44 games. After seven seasons in Montreal, Stewart was traded to Boston, where he scored his 200th NHL goal. In 1937, he won another goal-scoring race; the following year, his 13th season, Stewart banged in his 300th on St. Patrick's day in a 5–3 Americans' loss to the Rangers. He received a standing ovation. A few nights earlier, in anticipation of the 300th, Stewart was given a case of flat silverware and a cocktail set from hockey friends at the Montreal Forum. Stewart played his last game on March 24, 1940. It was the 650th of his career. He had scored 324 goals for 515 points and compiled a healthy 953 penalty minutes.

Nels Stewart was the NHL's first 300-goal scorer.

7.2   **C. Maurice Richard**
There have been more than 5,500 players in NHL history, but only 26 have hit the milestone 500-goal mark. Richard's big moment came on October 19, 1957, at the Montreal Forum. At 15:52 of the first period, linemate Jean Béliveau fed a pass to Richard, who slapped it past Chicago's Glenn Hall to become the NHL's first 500-goal scorer. The crowd roared and the organist played "Il a Gagne ses Epaulettes" (He's Earned His Stripes). It was Richard's 863rd game. Richard scored number 500 four years ahead of Gordie Howe's 500th, which came on March 14, 1962.

7.3   **A. Bobby Hull**
After Maurice Richard and Gordie Howe each scored their 500ths, in 1957 and 1962, it was another eight years before the NHL had its third 500-goal scorer, Bobby Hull. Hull notched number 500 in his 861st game (two games less than Richard) on February 21, 1970, against Ed Giacomin, in a 4–2 Chicago win over New York. Béliveau recorded number 500 a year later (February 11, 1971), followed by Mahovlich (March 21, 1973) and Esposito (December 22, 1974).

7.4   **B. One player**
American-born players began making inroads into the NHL in significant numbers during the 1970s and 1980s. Among those, few have had the impact of Joe Mullen, the only U.S.-born NHLer to score 500 goals. Born and raised in New York City, Mullen's 16-year NHL career has been a highlight reel of American firsts. Signed as a free agent by St. Louis in 1979, Mullen began his scoring spree by becoming the first player to record more than 20 goals in both the NHL (25 with St. Louis) and the minor leagues (21 with Salt Lake)—in the same season. In 1983–84, he set an NHL record for goals (41) by an American-born player. After his trade to Calgary, Mullen won the Lady Byng Trophy (1987, 1989) as most gentlemanly player— the first U.S.-born player to do so since 1936. In

1988–89, the New York native set a league record for points (110) by an American, becoming the second-oldest player to net a 50-goal season in NHL history. On January 13, 1990, Mullen scored his 686th point to pass Neal Broten as the all-time leading U.S.-born scorer. His other American firsts include: his 400th career goal (March 17, 1992), his 900th career point (February 27, 1993) and his 1,000th career point (February 7, 1995). Mullen played on three Cup winners (Calgary (1989) and Pittsburgh (1991, 1992), and was named to 1989's first All-Star team after leading the league in plus/minus with a +51. The first 500th goal by an American-born player was scored on a deflected shot past Colorado's Patrick Roy on March 14, 1997. As of 1997, other Americans prospects to join the 500-goal club include: Pat LaFontaine (445 goals), Jeremy Roenick (296), Mike Modano (256), Keith Tkachuk (196) and John LeClair (175).

7.5 **C. Gump Worsley**
During his long and sometimes tortured goaltending career, the Gumper suffered his share of adversity at the hands of some of hockey's greatest snipers. Few netminders want to be reminded of, or remembered as, the goalie that gave up "that important goal." It might be a simple shot in a heartbreaking loss; a devasting Stanley Cup loser; or a milestone goal forever recorded on the books. All the greats have endured the agony of waiting; watching opponents celebrate as the crowd roars and litters the ice in response to the momentous occasion. But Worsley seemed to attract indignities better than most, including a five-goal game courtesy of Bernie Geoffrion in 1955, Bobby Hull's first 50th goal in 1962 and two of Gordie Howe's most important milestone markers, his 500th on March 14, 1962, and, three year later, the NHL's first 600th goal on November 27, 1965. Worsley split the milestones between two teams: he was a Ranger for Howe's 500th, and a Canadien for his 600th.

MILESTONES: ANSWERS

7.6 **B. Johnny Bucyk**
Bucyk's longevity is almost as legendary as Gordie Howe's. He played in 1,540 NHL games over 23 seasons from 1955–56 to 1977–78. He broke in with Detroit, but after two ordinary seasons and very little ice time, the big winger was traded to Boston for All-Star goalie Terry Sawchuk. Although Bucyk had been named the Western Hockey League's rookie of the year in 1954, few knew of his full potential. In Boston, Bucyk flourished into a solidly consistent 20-goal scorer. He was a mainstay during the team's tough times and, when the Bruins became a powerhouse under Bobby Orr and Phil Esposito, Bucyk was named captain and became know as "Chief." His best season was 1970–71 when he scored 51 goals, the oldest NHLer ever to reach that standard. Steadily, he climbed to the 500-goal plateau, which he reached on October 30, 1975, in his 1,370th game. No player had taken so long, but no player deserved it more than Boston's "Chief."

7.7 **D. More than 40 years old**
Howe's epic career spanned five decades. During that time his name became associated with almost every hockey milestone, including the 100-point season. By the time Howe did it in his 1,548th game in March 1969, he was 41 years old—an astonishing 16 years older than the average age (25 years) of the almost 100 NHLers who've reached the 100-point mark.

7.8 **D. Phil Esposito**
During the 1940s, top players scored in the 70- to 80-point range. Then, in 1952–53, Gordie Howe cracked the 90-point barrier with an unprecedented 95 points. Under the right circumstances, with the right linemates, 100 points was finally feasible. Yet, even after expansion, 15 years later, with six new teams and a diluted talent pool, no one had hit 100. Finally, Phil Esposito, traded from Chicago to Boston, scored number 100 on March 2, 1969. The historic point came on a goal tucked underneath a sprawling Joe Daley in Boston's 4–0 win over

Pittsburgh. It was Espo's 60th game. By year's end, he had won the NHL scoring race with an amazing 49–77–126 record. After waiting so long for someone to break 100, the league had its hero. But Espo was not alone. Two other NHLers also scored 100 points that season, Bobby Hull and Gordie Howe.

7.9 **D. 11 games more**

Among Esposito's many "got-yas" directed at Chicago after his blockbuster trade from the Hawks, perhaps the sweetest came in 1969 when he became the NHL's first 100-point scorer. Espo had been Bobby Hull's centre on the Hawks and now the two rival stars were chasing the 100-point plateau. Esposito got there first in his 60th game of 1968–69,; Hull notched his 100th 11 games later in his 71st game, on March 20, 1969. Gordie Howe was the third NHLer to record a 100-point season, pegging his century mark on March 30, 1969, during his 76th game.

7.10 **B. Vic Hadfield**

Hadfield was the sixth NHLer to score 50 goals in a season, but he was the first to do it with more than 100 minutes in box time. The Ranger forward accumulated 142 penalty minutes and finished fourth in scoring with a 50–56–106 record in 1971–72. The first multiple 50-goal/100-PIM NHLer is Toronto's Rick Vaive, who in three straight seasons had records of 54 goals and 157 PIM (1981–82), 51 goals and 105 PIM (1982–83) and 52 goals and 114 PIM (1983–84).

7.11 **A. Jimmy Carson**

When Maurice Richard posted the NHL's first 50-goal season, he was 23 years old, as were Bobby Hull and Guy Lafleur when they first scored 50. But no one hit that benchmark at a younger age than Gretzky and Carson, who were the only teenagers to record 50-goal seasons in the NHL. Gretzky was 19 years and two months old, Carson was six months older. Gretzky scored his 50th in his 78th game of his first NHL season on April 2, 1980.

MILESTONES: ANSWERS

Carson netted number 50 on March 26, 1988, in his 77th game of his second season. Gretzky totalled 51 goals; Carson, 55.

The NHL's Youngest 50-Goal Scorers*

Player	Team	Date of 50th Goal	Game No.	Age
Wayne Gretzky	Edm	02–04–80	78	19.2
Jimmy Carson	LA	26–03–88	77	19.8
Pierre Larouche	Pit	03–04–76	75	20.5
Craig Simpson	Edm	15–03–88	71	21.1
Mike Bossy	NYI	01–04–78	69	21.2
Mark Messier	Edm	31–03–82	78	21.3
Mario Lemieux	Pit	12–03–87	53	21.5
Joe Nieuwendyk	Cal	12–03–88	66	21.5
Paul Kariya	Ana	14–04–96	82	21.5
Dino Ciccarelli	Min	08–03–82	67	21.7

*Current to 1997

7.12 D. Mike Bossy

Throughout Bossy's stellar career, he was forever in the shadows of Wayne Gretzky. The Islander sniper consistently produced 50-goal seasons for nine straight years (compared to Gretzky's nine in 17 seasons). But, typically, No. 99's off-the-chart numbers made every other scorer of his era a hockey footnote, no matter the feat. Bossy does have the edge in one category: his NHL-record nine straight 50-goal seasons is one better than Gretzky's eight in a row.

7.13 D. Five players

There is no prerequisite for joining the 500-goal club, except good health and long-term consistency as a goal scorer. A few 50-goal seasons certainly boost the career totals towards the half-century mark, but it's not always necessary. In fact, five of the NHL's most famous snipers— Gordie Howe, Jean Béliveau, Frank Mahovlich, Stan

Mikita and Gilbert Perreault—never notched a 50-goal year, despite having 500-goal careers.

7.14 C. Five players

The true 50-in-50 goal scorer should score 50 goals in his team's first 50 games of the season, rather than in the *player's* first 50 games of the season. An even stiffer test is the 50-in-less-than-50 category. Only five NHLers qualify. Wayne Gretzky did it three times, Mario Lemieux twice and Brett Hull, Alexander Mogilny and Cam Neely once each. How many among those five scored their 50th before their team's 50th game? Just Gretzky, Lemieux and Hull.

The NHL's 50-in-Less-Than-50 Goal Scorers*

Player	Team	Season	Date of 50th goal	Player Game No.	Team Game No.
Wayne Gretzky	Edm	1981–82	30–12–81	39	39
Wayne Gretzky	Edm	1983–84	07–01–84	42	42
Wayne Gretzky	Edm	1984–85	26–01–85	49	49
Mario Lemieux	Pit	1988–89	20–01–89	44	46
Brett Hull	StL	1990–91	25–01–91	49	49
Mario Lemieux	Pit	1992–93	21–03–93	48	72
Alex Mogilny	Buf	1992–93	03–02–93	46	53
Cam Neely	Bos	1993–94	07–03–94	44	66

*Current to 1997

7.15 B. Between 120 and 140 games

The Islanders' Mike Bossy is the fastest 100-goal scorer from the start of a career, notching goal number 100 during his 129th game in his second NHL season, 1978–79. Bossy scored 53 goals during his rookie campaign and then popped in his 47th of 1978–79 on February 19, 1979, for his 100th career goal. The next fastest NHLer to score 100 goals is Teemu Selanne, who missed Bossy's record by just one game, scoring his 100th in game num-

Maurice Richard was hockey's first 500-goal scorer.

ber 130 (January 12, 1994). Wayne Gretzky scored his 100th NHL goal into an empty net on March 7, 1981. It was Gretzky's 145th NHL match.

7.16 **A. Maurice Richard's career goal-scoring total**
They called him the Rocket and claimed he was the best player from the blueline in. On most nights, few would argue with that assessment. Darting into his opponent's

zone, Richard drove to the net with an intensity that struck fear into every goalie he faced. His glowing eyes widened to the size of chunks of black coal when he went in for the kill. Around the net, Richard was possessed. A pure goal scorer, he never tallied enough assists to win a scoring championship. But in Catholic Quebec, his homeland, that didn't matter. Richard was literally their other "God," registering five-goal games, winning Stanley Cups on overtime goals and causing riots in the streets of Montreal. He became the sniper others set their standards by. Richard recorded the NHL's first 50-in-50 season and reached the 500-goal plateau before anyone else. When he retired in 1960, he had 544 goals.

7.17 **D. 27 consecutive seasons**
Howe registered an NHL-record 22 consecutive 20-or-more-goal seasons and then another five straight in the WHA. Remarkably, Howe never missed scoring a 20-goal season in four decades between 1949–50 and 1977–78.

7.18 **D. Bobby: 861 games, Brett: 693 games**
Almost 27 years after Bobby Hull became only the third NHLer to score 500 goals, his son Brett became the 24th to reach the 500-club. Bobby notched his 500th in game number 861 on February 21, 1970, and Brett in game number 693 on December 22, 1996. Bobby and Brett are the only father-son combo in the 500-goal club.

7.19 **B. One game**
The crowd chanted "Mar-i-o, Mar-i-o, Mar-i-o" and threw hundreds of hats onto the ice as Lemieux acknowledged the standing ovation with a wave of his stick. The cheering continued while the video board replayed highlights from his 13-year career. Unlike number 500, Mario's 600th career goal was scored at home in Pittsburgh. "That's why I wanted to do it tonight. To get a standing ovation like that is something special," Lemieux said. The historic goal, an empty-netter, came in the last minute of play against Vancouver in the

Penguins 6–4 win on February 4, 1997. It was Mario's 719th career game, only one more game than it took Gretzky to score 600.

7.20 **D. 1) Howe, 2) Esposito, 3) Dionne, 4) Gretzky**
Gordie Howe became the first NHLer to score 700 career goals, in 1968–69. At 40 years old, he was in his 23rd NHL season. Esposito, 38, netted his 700th in 1979–80, his 17th season. Dionne was the NHL's third 700-goal scorer, recording his milestone marker during his 17th season in 1987–88, at age 36. Naturally, Gretzky scored goal number 700 the quickest of the group. The Great One was just 30 years old and in his 12th season. Mike Gartner is primed to become the fifth NHLer to score 700 goals, sometime in 1997–98.

7.21 **C. Steve Yzerman**
The third-youngest sniper to score 1,000 points after Gretzky (age 23) and Lemieux (age 26) is Yzerman, who notched number 1,000 during his 737th game on February 24, 1993. He was 27 years and nine months old, and in his 10th NHL season.

The NHL's Youngest 1,000-Point Scorers*

Player	Team	Date of 1000th	Game No.	Age
Wayne Gretzky	Edm	12/19/84	424	23.11
Mario Lemieux	Pit	03/24/92	513	26.5
Steve Yzerman	Det	02/24/93	737	27.9
Dale Hawerchuk	Buf	03/08/91	781	27.11
Mike Bossy	NYI	01/24/86	656	29.0
Denis Savard	Chi	03/11/90	727	29.2
Marcel Dionne	LA	01/07/81	740	29.5
Guy Lafleur	Mtl	03/04/81	720	29.5
Bryan Trottier	NYI	01/29/85	726	29.6
Paul Coffey	Pit	12/22/90	770	29.7

*Current to 1997

Game SEVEN

GAMES-PLAYED LEADERS

The hockey words and player names listed below appear in the puzzle horizontally, vertically or backwards. Some are easily found, like HOCKEY (spelled backwards); others require a more careful search. After you've circled all 42 words, read the remaining letters in descending order to spell the name of the NHLer who appears in our sketch. Only Gordie Howe played more NHL games than our mystery man. Who is he?

(Solutions are on page 138)

Allan Stanley • Abel • Bill Gadsby • Bryan Trottier • Dave Keon • Dean Prentice • Doug Mohns • Games • Goal • Gordie Howe • Harry Howell • Henri Richard • Hero • Honour • Jean Ratelle • John Bucyk • Larry Murphy • Larry Robinson • Leaders • Long • Loss • Marcel Dionne • Many • Mike Gartner • Mikita • Norm Ullman • Players • Phil Esposito • Ray Bourque • Red Kelly • Ron Stewart • Regular • Rove • Skate • Stamina • Stan • Strong • Time • Tim Horton • Uniform • Wayne Gretzky • Win

```
L M O T I S O P S E L I H P Y N A M
L A D E A N P R E N T I C E H W B I
E R R B I L L G A D S B Y N P A E K
W C A R K A S K A T E L O L R Y L I
O E H Y Y S T I M E A E G E U N M T
H L C A C R R E W O K O S U M E I A
Y D I N U E O I G E R X T Q Y G K L
R I R T B D N B V D N R A R R R E L
R O I R N A G A I A A U M U R E G A
A N R O H E D E M N T O I O A T A N
H N N T O L H L D E S N N B L Z R S
E E E T J O L G N O L O A Y O K T T
R L H I W U (Y E K C O H) N A S Y N A
O V S E M A G R A L U G E R S   E N
N O T R O H M I T Y L L E K D E R L
C R O N S T E W A R T C H I R O V E
S N H O M G U O D O M R O F I N U Y
E L L E T A R N A E J S R E Y A L P
```

Chapter EIGHT

THE CHART TOPPERS

The NHL's first scoring leader was Joe Malone. In the league's inaugural season, 1917–18, Malone set a torrid scoring pace, averaging more than two goals per game during the 22-game regular season. On the strength of multiple three-, four- and five-goal games, he potted 44 goals (in 20 games), establishing a still-standing league record. To equal Malone's 2.20 goals-per-game ratio today, an NHLer would have to net 180 goals in the 82-game schedule. *(Answers are on page 116)*

8.1 Which sniper has led the NHL in goal scoring the most times?
  A. Gordie Howe
  B. Bobby Hull
  C. Phil Esposito
  D. Wayne Gretzky

8.2 Who was the first NHL scoring leader to accumulate more than 100 penalty minutes in a season?
  A. Frank Nighbor
  B. Reg Noble
  C. Odie Cleghorn
  D. Nels Stewart

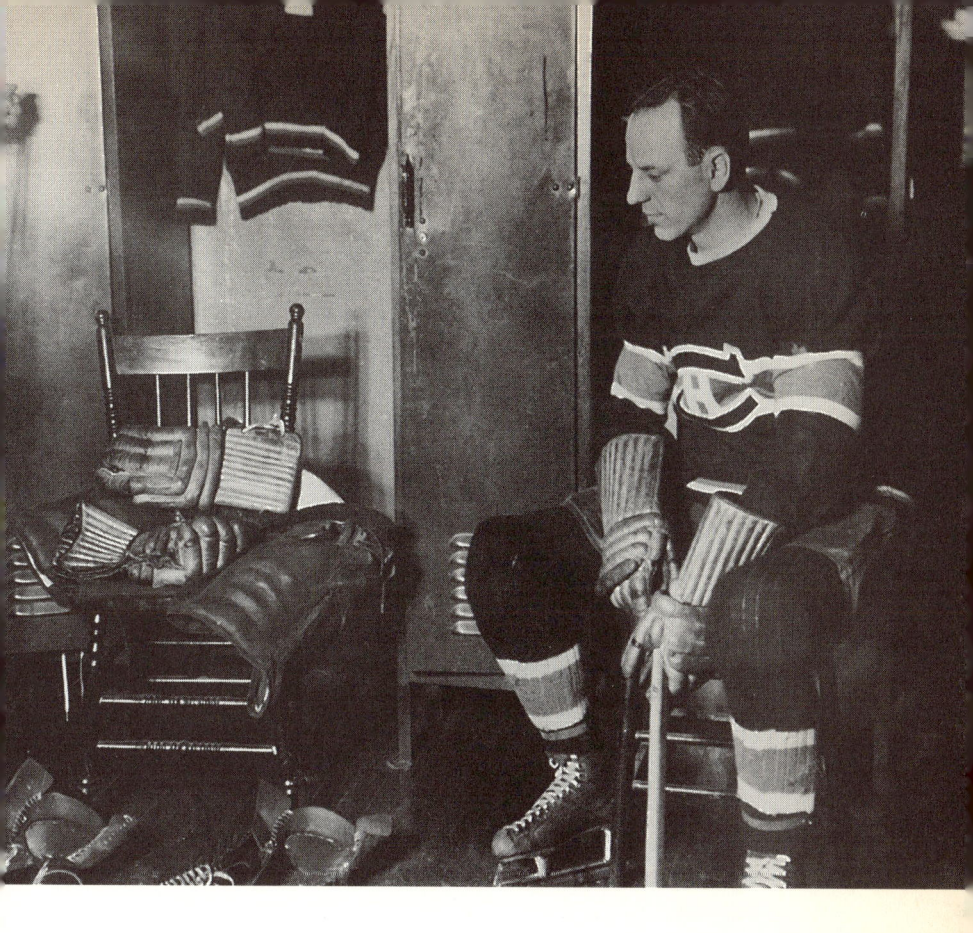

8.3 **In the picture above, whose equipment is in the chair next to Aurel Joliat in the Montreal Canadiens dressing room?**
A. Georges Vezina's
B. Howie Morenz's
C. Toe Blake's
D. Larry Robinson's

8.4 **Who was the first NHLer to lead the league in goals and amass more than 200 penalty minutes in the same season?**
A. Detroit's Brendan Shanahan
B. Chicago's Al Secord
C. Phoenix's Keith Tkachuk
D. Pittsburgh's Kevin Stevens

8.5 Which career goal-scoring leader held his title the longest?
A. Howie Morenz
B. Gordie Howe
C. Maurice Richard
D. Wayne Gretzky

8.6 Who were the first brothers to win NHL scoring titles?
A. Bobby and Dennis Hull
B. Charlie and Roy Conacher
C. Max and Doug Bentley
D. Maurice and Henri Richard

8.7 Who is the only NHL scoring leader to be traded the season after he won his title?
A. Max Bentley
B. Wayne Gretzky
C. Phil Esposito
D. Ted Lindsay

8.8 Which two players share the record for the highest season point total prior to 1967 expansion? What was the total?
A. Gordie Howe and Dickie Moore—95 points
B. Gordie Howe and Bernie Geoffrion—97 points
C. Stan Mikita and Bobby Hull—97 points
D. Phil Esposito and Bobby Hull—99 points

8.9 Which sniper tied Bobby Hull for most points in 1961–62, but lost the Art Ross Trophy as scoring leader because Hull had more goals?
A. Gordie Howe
B. Stan Mikita
C. Frank Mahovlich
D. Andy Bathgate

THE CHART TOPPERS: QUESTIONS

8.10 What is the greatest number of players to tie for the NHL goal-scoring lead in one season?
A. Two players
B. Three players
C. Four players
D. Five players

8.11 What is the greatest number of defensemen to rank among the NHL's top 10 scorers in one season?
A. One defenseman
B. Two defensemen
C. Three defensemen
D. Four defensemen

8.12 Which is the only NHL team in league history to have the top four scorers in one season?
A. The Pittsburgh Penguins
B. The Boston Bruins
C. The Edmonton Oilers
D. The Montreal Canadiens

8.13 Who was the first scoring leader to win an NHL scoring race by potting more assists than goals?
A. Bill Cook
B. Charlie Conacher
C. Ace Bailey
D. Sweeney Schriner

8.14 Who was the last scoring leader to win an NHL scoring race by registering more goals than assists?
A. Phil Esposito
B. Bobby Hull
C. Gordie Howe
D. Bill Cowley

Answers

THE CHART TOPPERS

8.1 **B. Bobby Hull**

During his prime, Hull was not only the NHL's most powerful skater, he also possessed the hardest shot. His high-velocity slapper was once timed at a terrifying 118.3 m.p.h. Those skills helped the Golden Jet top the NHL in goal scoring a record seven times in his career. It's possible Hull would have won more NHL goal-scoring races had he not jumped to the WHA in 1972–73. In 1974–75, he blasted in a WHA-record 77 goals with the Winnipeg Jets.

The NHL's Top Goal-Scoring Champs*

Player	Team	Titles
Bobby Hull	Chicago	7
Phil Esposito	Boston	6
Wayne Gretzky	Edmonton	5
Maurice Richard	Montreal	5
Charlie Conacher	Toronto	5
Gordie Howe	Detroit	5
Mario Lemieux	Pittsburgh	3
Brett Hull	St. Louis	3
Babe Dye	Ham/Tor	3
Bill Cook	NYR	3

*Current to 1997

8.2 **D. Nels Stewart**

They didn't call Stewart "Old Poison" for nothing. The deadly accuracy of his shot earned him his nickname, the 1925–26 scoring title (42 points) and 119 penalty minutes that season. It was the first time an NHL scoring leader had

Bobby Hull and some young admirers.

more than 100 penalty minutes in a year. True, the league was only nine years old, but Stewart was just one minor penalty shy of the league-leading 121 minutes collected by tough guy Bert Corbeau. Stewart wanted to make an impression and indeed he did. It was his rookie year.

8.3 **B. Howie Morenz's**
During the 1920s and 1930s, there was no offensive force in hockey that rivalled Howie Morenz. His wicked shot and flamboyant skating style made him a million-dollar box-office attraction. American writers called him the Babe Ruth of hockey, and, like Ruth, Morenz played hard and lived fast. During his best years, he won two scoring titles, both with left-winger Aurel Joliat on the Canadiens' Speedball Line. But in 1937, Morenz suffered a leg injury that hospitalized him; he died soon after of complications. Tens of thousands of mourners attended his funeral at the Montreal Forum. Joliat played another season, but clearly he missed his linemate and partner of 12 years. Morenz and Joliat were the original Flying Frenchmen of the Canadiens. Their goal-scoring records are identical: each scored 270 goals.

8.4 C. Phoenix's Keith Tkachuk

Although a few players share the distinction of putting together seasons of 30-goal, 300–PIM stats or 50–250, no one but Tkachuk can claim winning the goal-scoring race with more than 200 minutes in the box. In fact, only five other goal-scoring leaders have amassed 100 penalty minutes or more, the next-highest being Jean Béliveau, a distant 85 minutes behind Tkachuk. Tkachuk became the first NHLer to accomplish the feat in 1996–97, with a league-high 52 goals and a team-leading 228 penalty minutes. Said Tkachuk: "The bottom line is I get paid well to play this game, I'm supposed to be the captain of this team and I can't play average."

The Highest PIM Totals by NHL Goal-Scoring Leaders*

Player	Team	Year	Games	Goals	PIM
Keith Tkachuk	Pho	1996–97	81	52	228
Jean Béliveau	Mtl	1955–56	70	47	143
Maurice Richard	Mtl	1954–55	67	38	125
Nels Stewart	MtlM	1925–26	36	34	119
Maurice Richard	Mtl	1949–50	70	43	114
Maurice Richard	Mtl	1953–54	70	37	112
Gordie Howe	Det	1962–63	70	38	100
Mario Lemieux	Pit	1988–89	76	85	100
Ted Lindsay	Det	1947–48	60	33	95
Mario Lemieux	Pit	1987–88	77	70	92

*Current to 1997

8.5 B. Gordie Howe

There have only been seven career goal-scoring champs in NHL history. In 1994, Gretzky, the seventh, took over from Howe, who had owned the NHL crown since dethroning Maurice Richard in 1963–64, 21 seasons earlier. No champ has held the title longer than Howe.

THE CHART TOPPERS: ANSWERS

The NHL's Career Goal-Scoring Champs*

Player	Year Record Set	Goals	Length of Reign
Joe Malone	1917–18	44	1 year
Cy Denneny	1918–19	54	1 year
Joe Malone	1919–20	146	4 years
Cy Denneny	1922–23	246	12 years
Howie Morenz	1933–34	270	4 years
Nels Stewart	1936–37	324	16 years
Maurice Richard	1952–53	544	12 years
Gordie Howe	1963–64	801	21 years
Wayne Gretzky	1993–94	861	3 years

*Current to 1997

8.6 C. Max and Doug Bentley

The Bentleys were not only the first siblings to win NHL scoring titles, they were also the first two Chicago Blackhawks to win the crown. Doug became Chicago's first NHL scoring champ in 1942–43; Max followed with two straight crowns for the Hawks in 1945–46 and 1946–47. The Conacher family is the only other hockey family to produce scoring-leader brothers: Charlie in 1933–34 and 1934–35 with Toronto, and Roy in 1948–49 with Chicago.

8.7 A. Max Bentley

Despite winning back-to-back NHL scoring titles with the Blackhawks in 1945–46 and 1946–47, Bentley was traded by Chicago after just six games in 1947–48. Winless in all six starts, Chicago was desperate for more depth. It produced the biggest deal in NHL history as Bentley, along with Cy Thomas, was traded to Toronto for Gus Bodnar, Bud Poile, Gaye Stewart, Bob Goldham and Ernie Dickens. Bentley never won another scoring race, but he probably didn't mind, considering he won three Stanley Cups with the Maple Leafs.

8.8 **C. Stan Mikita and Bobby Hull—97 points**
During the NHL's six-team era, no player cracked the 100-point barrier. Each season the elusive mark remained a challenge for "next season." Players came agonizingly close: Gordie Howe and Bernie Geoffrion had 95 points in 1952–53 and 1960–61; and Dickie Moore raised the stakes with his 96-point season in 1958–59. The closest was 97 points, scored by Bobby Hull and Stan Mikita in 1965–66 and 1966–67, the last two years of the six-team era.

8.9 **D. Andy Bathgate**
One of hockey's great gunners, Bathgate possessed every innate skill of a true superstar. In fact, his command of the game borrowed from the best: the grace of a Béliveau; the slap shot of a Hull; the strength of a Howe; and the pinpoint passes of a Gretzky. Unfortunately, Bathgate also had the cranky knees of an Orr. Yet, with a steel plate in one knee and, as Ranger goalie Gump Worsley observed, "a prayer in the other," Bathgate endured 1,069 games over 17 NHL seasons. His spirit showed in every game and his generosity as a playmaker was displayed on every shift. Bathgate's greatest season came in 1958–59, when he tallied 88 points and won the Hart Trophy as league MVP. In 1961–62, he equalled Bobby Hull with 84 points in league scoring, but Hull was awarded the Art Ross Trophy based on most goals scored. Hull had a 50-34-84 record versus Bathgate's 28-56-84. It was the first time a scoring title had ever been decided by most goals.

8.10 **B. Three players**
There have been seven ties for goal-scoring leader in NHL history. On six occasions two players tied. The other year, 1979–80, three players—Charlie Simmer, Danny Gare and Blaine Stoughton—all recorded the season's highest goal count (56 goals). On two occasions, in 1935–36 and 1954–55, two teammates tied for first in the goal-scoring race.

The NHL's "Tied" Goal-Scoring Leaders*

Year	Player	Team	Goals
1931–32	Charlie Conacher	Toronto	34
	Bill Cook	Rangers	34
1935–36	Charlie Conacher	Toronto	23
	Bill Thoms	Toronto	23
1936–37	Larry Aurie	Detroit	23
	Nels Stewart	Maroons	23
1954–55	Maurice Richard	Montreal	38
	Bernie Geoffrion	Montreal	38
1959–60	Bobby Hull	Chicago	39
	Bronco Horvath	Boston	39
1979–80	Charlie Simmer	Los Angeles	56
	Danny Gare	Buffalo	56
	Blaine Stoughton	Hartford	56
1992–93	Teemu Selanne	Winnipeg	76
	Alex Mogilny	Buffalo	76

*Current to 1997

8.11 **B. Two defensemen**
Bobby Orr, Paul Coffey, Ray Bourque and Brian Leetch all cracked the NHL's top 10 scoring list during their careers, but only once in league history have two blueliners managed it in the same season. In 1973–74, Orr came second (to Phil Esposito) with 122 points, and the Rangers' Brad Park finished tied for tenth with 82 points.

8.12 **B. The Boston Bruins**
Numerous records were shattered during the 1970–71 season, many by members of the Bruins, who boasted the NHL's top four scorers and six of the top eight. Boston's depth was staggering; its scoring force overwhelming. Bobby Orr cracked the 100-assist barrier with 102 assists; Phil Esposito set league records ablaze, firing in 76 goals for 152 points. The Bruins were so talent-rich that 35-year-old Johnny Bucyk, playing left wing on the second

line, scored 51 goals. In all, Boston netted an NHL-record 399 goals. Boston's dominance can be judged by another factor: longevity. Three years later, in 1973–74, four Bruins again swept the top four places in the scoring parade.

The NHL's Leading Scorers in 1970–71

Player	Team	GP	G	A	PTS
Phil Esposito	Bos	78	76	76	152
Bobby Orr	Bos	78	37	102	139
John Bucyk	Bos	78	51	65	116
Ken Hodge	Bos	78	43	62	105
Bobby Hull	Chi	78	44	52	96
Norm Ullman	Tor	73	34	51	85
Wayne Cashman	Bos	77	21	58	79
John McKenzie	Bos	65	31	46	77

8.13 D. Sweeney Schriner

If there is any statistical reference (besides goal-scoring volume) that illustrates the difference in the hockey played by scoring champions of the 1920s and 1930s and the players of today, it might be the goal-assist ratio. Unlike current scoring leaders who consistently pile up more assists than goals to win championships, in hockey's early era all point-scoring champs won their titles with a higher goal count. In 1923–24, Cy Denneny won the league scoring race, compiling a 22–1–23 record in the 24-game schedule. This ratio, though skewed, seems due more to officiating than the style of play. In old-time hockey, assists were strictly awarded, based usually on a direct pass. There was no forward passing allowed inside the attacking zone, and it's unclear if drop passes counted as an assist. Also, until 1926 there was only one on-ice official, a referee, to watch all the action. But with the changes in offside rules and forward passing (and the three-man on-ice officiating crew), the flow of the game

Stan Mikita shaping his "banana blade."

opened up and players began increasing their assist totals. The first player to win a scoring race with a better assist than goal mark was Sweeney Schriner, who netted 19 goals and 26 assists in 1935–36. Since then, only six players have won the NHL scoring race with a higher goal than assist count.

8.14 B. Bobby Hull

As of 1997, no one has won a scoring championship with more goals than assists since Bobby did it in 1965–66, when he compiled a 54–43–97 record. Phil Esposito follows a close second after his 76–76–152 record-setting season of 1970–71. Other scoring champs who recorded a higher goal than assist mark include Gordie Howe, Bernie Geoffrion and Max Bentley.

OLD-TIMER TOTALS

Listed below, in chronological order, are the NHL records of 16 veterans with 10 to 26 years of experience. Using the years, games played and point totals or PIM as clues, match the records to the players in the following four columns. *(Solutions are on page 139)*

Mike Bossy	Johnny Bucyk	Bobby Clarke	Babe Dye
Rod Gilbert	Doug Harvey	Tim Horton	Gordie Howe
Bobby Hull	Howie Morenz	Don Marshall	Bobby Orr
Brad Park	Dean Prentice	Jean Ratelle	Steve Shutt

Player	Years	GP	G	A	PTS	PIM
1._____	10	752	573	553	1,126	210
2._____	11	269	202	42	243	205
3._____	12	657	270	645	915	953
4._____	13	930	424	393	817	410
5._____	14	550	270	197	467	563
6._____	15	1,144	358	852	1,210	1,453
7._____	16	1,063	610	560	1,170	640
8._____	17	1,113	213	683	896	1,429
9._____	18	1,065	406	615	1,021	508
10._____	19	1,176	265	324	589	127
11._____	20	1,113	88	452	540	1,216
12._____	21	1,281	491	776	1,267	276
13._____	22	1,378	391	469	863	484
14._____	23	1,540	556	813	1,369	497
15._____	24	1,446	115	403	518	1,611
16._____	26	1,767	801	1,049	1,846	1,675

Chapter NINE

STANLEY CUP SHARPSHOOTERS

What is the highest goal count by one player in a Stanley Cup final series? Three players—Jean Béliveau, Mike Bossy and Wayne Gretzky—registered seven goals. But two other NHLers have scored more goals in finals action. One is Alf Skinner of the Toronto Arenas, who notched eight goals in 1918's five-game final against Vancouver. The other player was the hero of Toronto's 1922 Stanley Cup championship. You'll find his name in the answer to question eight in this chapter, which is devoted to the goal scorers and point earners who made their mark in the Stanley Cup playoffs.

(Answers are on page 128)

9.1 **As of 1997, who holds the NHL record for most playoff goals?**
A. Jari Kurri
B. Maurice Richard
C. Wayne Gretzky
D. Mark Messier

9.2 **Who owns the NHL record for the most points in one playoff series?**
A. Pittsburgh's Mario Lemieux
B. Toronto's Doug Gilmour
C. Edmonton's Wayne Gretzky
D. Boston's Rick Middleton

THE GOAL SCORERS

9.3 What is the greatest number of goals scored by a team in one playoff series?
A. 22 goals
B. 33 goals
C. 44 goals
D. 55 goals

9.4 What is the greatest number of goals scored by one player in one playoff series?
A. Six goals
B. Eight goals
C. 10 goals
D. 12 goals

9.5 Which two players share the record for most goals scored in one playoff year?
A. Mike Bossy and Joe Sakic
B. Reggie Leach and Jari Kurri
C. Wayne Gretzky and Kevin Stevens
D. Mark Messier and Steve Payne

9.6 Which player recorded the most game-winning goals in one playoff season?
A. The Canadiens' Jean Béliveau, in 1965
B. The Bruins' Bobby Orr, in 1972
C. The Islanders' Mike Bossy, in 1983
D. The Avalanche's Joe Sakic, in 1996

9.7 In what year did the NHL produce its first 20-point playoff scorer? Who was he?
A. 1934–35
B. 1944–45
C. 1954–55
D. 1964–65

9.8 What is the greatest number of goals scored by one player in a Stanley Cup final series?
A. Eight goals
B. Nine goals

C. 10 goals
D. 11 goals

9.9 Which Montreal Canadiens player holds the NHL record for the most goals scored in the Stanley Cup finals?
A. Maurice Richard
B. Jean Béliveau
C. Bernie Geoffrion
D. Yvan Cournoyer

9.10 Whose playoff record of 17 goals did Reggie Leach break when he scored 19 times during the 1976 playoffs?
A. Bobby Hull
B. Frank Mahovlich
C. Phil Esposito
D. Newsy Lalonde

9.12 How many players have scored more than one Stanley Cup-winning goal?
A. Two players, Maurice Richard and Bobby Orr
B. Three players
C. Four players
D. Six players

9.11 What is the fastest time a Stanley Cup-winning goal was scored from the start of a game?
A. In less than a minute
B. Between the 1:00- and 5:00-minute marks
C. Between the 5:00- and 10:00-minute marks
D. After more than 10 minutes

9.13 How many playoff MVPs scored their team's Stanley Cup-winning goal?
A. One player, Wayne Gretzky
B. Three players
C. Five players
D. Seven players

Answers

STANLEY CUP SHARPSHOOTERS

9.1 C. Wayne Gretzky

The NHL record for most playoff goals has long been a three-way battle among former Oiler teammates, Gretzky, Messier and Kurri. Typically, Gretzky leads the pack with 122 playoff goals, followed by Messier's 109. The Great One reached double digits in goals scored five times and had his best season in 1984–85, when he totaled 17 goals in 18 games. Gretzky has never failed to score in any playoff year in which he's participated. His scoring average after 209 playoff games is a whopping 58 per cent.

The NHL's Top Playoff Goal Scorers*

Player	Teams	Years	GP	Goals
Wayne Gretzky	Edm/LA/StL/NYR	1980–97	208	122
Mark Messier	Edm/NYR	1980–97	236	109
Jari Kurri	Edm/LA/NYR/Ana	1981–97	196	106
Glenn Anderson	Edm/Tor/NYR/StL	1981–97	225	93
Mike Bossy	NYI	1978–87	129	85
Maurice Richard	Mtl	1944–60	133	82

*Current to 1997

9.2 D. Boston's Rick Middleton

No sniper in NHL history has produced more points in one playoff series than Middleton, who in 1982–83 scored 19 points on five goals and 14 assists in the seven-game division finals against Buffalo. Middleton recorded six multiple-point games, his best coming in game five on

April 20, when he netted six points (a Boston playoff record) in a 9–0 rout of the Sabres.

9.3 **C. 44 goals**

This record belongs to the powerhouse Oiler teams of the 1980s, who featured Gretzky, Messier, Kurri and Coffey in their prime, playing firewagon hockey. No team has ever turned on red lights faster than Edmonton. In 1985's Western Conference finals, the Oilers' offensive juggernaut averaged 7.3 goals per game, outscoring Chicago 44–25 through six games of the best-of-seven series. In that playoff round, Edmonton notched two double-digit games, an NHL first in modern history. Trying to stem the puck parade was Hawk goalie Murray Bannerman, who earned the distinction of allowing the most playoff goals in one series in Chicago's 70-year history. On offense, the Blackhawks, with Denis Savard, Steve Larmer and Doug Wilson, combined to average more than four goals per game. The Oilers–Hawks series shootout produced an NHL record: the most goals by both teams in one playoff series, 11.5 goals per game. Which player scored the most goals? The answer, revealed in the next answer, is another league record.

The NHL's Highest-Scoring Playoff Series
1985 Western Conference Finals • Edmonton–Chicago

May 4	Chicago 2 at Edmonton 11
May 7	Chicago 3 at Edmonton 7
May 9	Edmonton 2 at Chicago 5
May 12	Edmonton 6 at Chicago 8
May 14	Chicago 5 at Edmonton 10
May 16	Edmonton 8 at Chicago 2

9.4 D. 12 goals

The 1985 Edmonton-Chicago Western Conference finals witnessed the highest goal production of any NHL playoff series. A league-record 69 goals were scored, with the Oilers outscoring the Hawks 44–25 in the six-game series. Individual NHL records were established, including Jari Kurri's 12-goal performance, the highest goal count in one playoff series. Kurri had two hat tricks and a four-goal game during the playoff round, another NHL record.

9.5 B. Reggie Leach and Jari Kurri

Leach and Kurri each scored 19 goals in their respective record-setting playoff seasons: Leach netting his 19 in 16 games during Philadelphia's 1976 postseason run to the Cup finals, and Kurri equalling that mark nine years later when Edmonton won the Cup in 18 games in 1985.

9.6 D. The Avalanche's Joe Sakic, in 1996

Sakic won more than an NHL championship when he hoisted the Stanley Cup and Conn Smythe Trophies in 1996, he finally won long overdue recognition as a true star. Quietly labouring for seven seasons with the lacklustre Quebec Nordiques, Sakic compiled a staggering 622 points in 508 games. Then, on the eve of greatness, the Nordiques became the Avalanche in Denver. The move brought Sakic his best season ever, as he finished third in league scoring with 51 goals and 69 assists. But his biggest test came in the postseason. And he was mesmerizing, scoring 18 goals in 22 playoff games—one shy of the record, and posting the most game-winners (six goals) in NHL history. The entire hockey world had finally noticed the scoring power of quiet Joe Sakic.

9.7 C. 1954–55

Although today's leading playoff scorers average about 30 points over a 20-game postseason, during the six-team era, Cup contenders played one semifinal round and one final series, usually scoring a high of 10 to 15 goals in about 10 to 12 games. In fact, from the NHL's inaugural season, 1917–18, to expansion in 1967–68, only two players scored 20 or more points in the postseason. Stan Mikita of Chicago had a 6-15-21 record in 12 games in 1961–62, and Detroit's Gordie Howe recorded the league's first 20-point playoff year in 1954–55. Since 1969–70, no leading point earner has scored less than 20 points in playoff action.

9.8 **B. Nine goals**
The record for most goals in a final series belongs to Cecil "Babe" Dye, hero of the 1921–22 Cup-champion Toronto St. Pats. Dye had been a star punter in Canadian football and a formidable baseball player, once receiving a $25,000 contract offer from the Philadelphia Athletics, but hockey proved a more difficult challenge. Dye was not a fast skater, yet he turned heads with his wicked shot and stickhandling finesse. Those skills earned him a spot on the St. Pats. Once there, Dye soon made his mark, winning two NHL scoring titles, notching two five-goal games and producing two 11-game goal-scoring streaks. But it's his playoff record that still stands today, an incredible nine-goal outburst in the 1922 final series against the Vancouver Millionaires. Dye scored five times in the first four games of the best-of-five series. In the fifth and deciding game, with the Stanley Cup up for grabs, Dye left nothing to chance. He exploded for four goals to salt the championship for Toronto in the 5–1 victory. Dye shares the NHL record with Ted Lindsay and Maurice Richard for most goals (4) in a final series game, but he is the only player in NHL history to score that often in a Cup-winning game.

9.9 **A. Maurice Richard**
The Montreal Canadiens have no fewer than six players atop the chart of finals' goal scorers. One of hockey's best playoff performers ever, Maurice Richard, scored a league-leading 34 goals in 12 Cup finals between 1944 and 1960. Although many of Richard's records have been shattered by Howe, Bossy and Gretzky, no one, other

than fellow Canadien Jean Béliveau, approaches his goal-scoring prowess in Cup final action.

The NHL's Highest-Scoring Finals' Snipers*

Player	Team	Games	Record	Goals
Maurice Richard	Mtl	59	34–12–46	34
Jean Béliveau	Mtl	65	30–32–62	30
Bernie Geoffrion	Mtl	53	22–24–46	24
Yvan Cournoyer	Mtl	50	21–19–40	21
Henri Richard	Mtl	65	21–26–47	21
Jacques Lemaire	Mtl	40	19–18–37	19
Gordie Howe	Det	55	18–32–50	18
Ted Lindsay	Det	44	18–14–32	18
Wayne Gretzky	Edm/LA	31	18–35–53	18
Mike Bossy	NYI	23	17–17–34	17

*Current to 1997

9.10 D. Newsy Lalonde

Lalonde racked up 17 goals in 10 games with the Montreal Canadiens during the 1919 playoffs. The fiery Habs forward netted 11 goals in the five-game NHL finals versus Ottawa, then added six more in the Stanley Cup final series against the Pacific Coast Hockey Association-champion Seattle Metropolitans. That series was suspended after five games due to an influenza outbreak. At that point, both clubs had posted two wins, with one game tied. Had the series run its full course, Lalonde likely would have added a few more goals to his total. In fact, he might still own the playoff goal-scoring record. Even so, Lalonde's mark lasted an incredible 57 years before Reggie Leach of the Philadelphia Flyers finally smashed it in 1976, when he bagged 19 goals in 16 playoff games.

Bobby Orr and Henri Richard. They both scored two Cup winners.

9.11 D. Six players

Between 1927 and 1997, six players have twice scored Stanley Cup winners. Predictably, the 24-time champion Montreal Canadiens have four players in the illustrious category. No NHLer has ever scored a Cup winner for two different teams.

Two-Time Cup-Winning Goal Scorers*

Player	Team	First Year	Second Year
Toe Blake	Montreal	1944	1946
Jean Béliveau	Montreal	1960	1965
Henri Richard	Montreal	1966	1971
Bobby Orr	Boston	1970	1972
Jacques Lemaire	Montreal	1977	1979
Mike Bossy	Islanders	1982	1983

*Current to 1997

9.12 **A. In less than a minute**
The NHL's top teams of 1964–65 squared off in a classic finals showdown that pitted the Béliveau-led Canadiens against Hull's Blackhawks. Through the first six games, the home teams won every contest. The seventh and deciding match, played at the Montreal Forum, completed the trend as Montreal routed Chicago 4–0 after a four-goal flurry in the first period. The Canadiens hit hard and early, possibly sensing Chicago's inexperience in seventh-game confrontations. (This was the club's first in franchise history.) The defining moment might have come when captain Jean Béliveau stunned the Hawk defense and sailed in on Glenn Hall to score at 0:14 seconds. The game's tone was set. Chicago reeled and Montreal's offense took advantage, adding three more goals to pad its first-period lead and secure the championship. During that seven-game final round, Béliveau had three game-winning goals and set up the fourth.

9.13 **C. Five players**
Since the Conn Smythe Trophy was first introduced in 1965, five players can lay claim to scoring the Cup winner and also being named playoff MVP. Jean Béliveau, who scored the Cup-winning goal for Montreal as part of his amazing five-goal, 10-point performance during 1965's seven-game final series against Chicago, was named the NHL's inaugural postseason MVP. Bobby Orr potted two Cup winners and snagged Conn Smythes for Boston in 1970 and 1972. Yvan Cournoyer was honoured as 1973's playoff MVP, when he scored an NHL-record 15 playoff goals, including the Cup winner (his second of two game-winning tallies in the Montreal–Chicago finals). Mike Bossy netted the Islanders' Cup winner in 1982, and took home the Conn Smythe after scoring seven goals in the four-game final against Vancouver. In 1988, Wayne Gretzky scored Edmonton's Cup winner, claimed playoff MVP status and established the league record for most points (13) in the finals.

Game SOLUTIONS

GAME 1: HALL OF FAME NICKNAMES

Part 1
1. Maurice Richard — D. "The Rocket"
2. Eric Lindros — J. "The Next One"
3. Lionel Conacher — F. "The Big Train"
4. Marcel Dionne — C. "Little Beaver"
5. Aurel Joliat — H. "The Mighty Atom"
6. Mike Bossy — I. "Boss"
7. Yvan Cournoyer — A. "The Roadrunner"
8. Johnny Bucyk — E. "Chief"
9. Emile Bouchard — G. "Butch"
10. Jeremy Roenick — B. "J. R."

Part 2
1. Mark Messier — G. "Moose"
2. Cecil Dye — C. "Babe"
3. Pavel Bure — A. "The Russian Rocket"
4. Frank Nighbor — H. "The Flying Dutchman"
5. Bernie Geoffrion — B. "Boom-Boom"
6. Ted Kennedy — D. "Teeder"
7. Guy Lafleur — J. "Flower"
8. Gordie Howe — I. "Mr. Hockey"
9. Harvey Jackson — F. "Busher"
10. Mario Lemieux — E. "Le Magnifique"

Part 3
1. Bobby Hull — I. "The Golden Jet"
2. Jaromir Jagr — G. "The Human Highlight Reel"
3. Alex Delvecchio — D. "Fats"
4. Hector Blake — F. "Toe"
5. Brett Hull — A. "The Golden Brett"
6. Nels Stewart — C. "Old Poison"
7. Max Bentley — J. "The Dipsy-Doodle Dandy of Delisle."
8. Henri Richard — B. "The Pocket Rocket"
9. Fred Taylor — H. "Cyclone"
10. Eddie Shore — E. "The Edmonton Express"

Part 4
1. Wayne Gretzky — D. "The Great One"
2. Frank Mahovlich — E. "The Big M"
3. Larry Robinson — G. "Big Bird"
4. Mel Hill — J. "Sudden Death"
5. Reggie Leach — C. "The Rifle"
6. Jack Stewart — A. "Black Jack"
7. Pierre Larouche — B. "Lucky Pierre"
8. Bryan Trottier — I. "Trots"
9. Edouard Lalonde — H. "Newsy"
10. Jean Béliveau — F. "Le Gros Bill"

THE GOAL SCORERS

GAME 2: ROOKIE SNIPERS

```
A Y-N R-E-N-B S E
M N L T-R-E T I S U
R R-A G-S-A-M H T-X
E M N D-R-E E L A-E
Z R-E O L-A-P-P U R
Y N A-V S N-U-T Y R
E L-I R Y I S T N E
T-O-R E S E-R-E T P
E B N D K S U S-A-T
O G I E-P Y O W G S
N R T-A-N-N D B E N
U S L R R H E N O-U
T E-O-R A O A E-L Y
S I-N-D H M B W I-L
  L K-U C-R-E I-T-A
```

Joe Nieuwendyk
Dale Hawerchuk
Peter Stastny
Steve Larmer
Pierre Turgeon
Luc Robitaille
Ray Sheppard
Eric Lindros
Teemu Selanne
Darryl Sutter
Neal Broten
Eric Vail
Mario Lemieux

Barry Pederson
Anton Stastny
Gil Perreault
Rick Martin
Steve Yzerman
Warren Young
Mikael Renberg

GAME 3: RETIRED NUMBERS

No. 2
Eddie Shore
Doug Harvey

No. 4
Bobby Orr
Jean Béliveau

No. 5
Bill Barilko
Denis Potvin

No. 7
Howie Morenz
Ted Lindsay
Rod Gilbert
Bill Barber
Phil Esposito

No. 9
Maurice Richard
Gordie Howe
Bobby Hull
Johnny Bucyk
Lanny McDonald

No. 16
Henri Richard
Marcel Dionne
Bobby Clarke
Michel Goulet

No. 10
Alex Delvecchio
Guy Lafleur

No. 11
Gil Perreault
Brian Sutter

No. 12
Sid Abel
Stan Smyl

No. 18
Dave Taylor

No. 21
Stan Mikita

No. 22
Mike Bossy

GAME SOLUTIONS

GAME 4: TEAM GOAL-LEADERS

```
  S-R-E-D-N-A-S-U-G
  N-O-L-O-N-I-R-E-D-O-N
  E-D-A-S-N-A-Y-R-U-F-A
  A-S-N-E-M-S-O-M-E-L-T
  D-M-Y-L-O-H-D-A-N-O-O
  M-A-T-H-A-N-E-P-D-R-E
  S-R-F-E-R-N-T-P-R-C-P
  H-Y-A-S-H-R-N-E-A-C-A
    I-M-E-L-I-A-E-H-L
  U-E-U-S-N-R-A-I-E-M-F
  X-N-I-N-O-U-N-A-L-A-F
  S-D-D-N-D-C-E-L-C-A-Y
  A-R-O-E-L-U-L-L-H-M-N
  N-A-B-T-A-H-R-A-S-E-A
  I-L-E-T-I-E-N-S-C-C-H
  K-U-G-K-E-R-I-E-C-I-S
  H-C-A-T-I-L-L-R-A
```

Ray Sheppard
Ray Ferraro
Mike Modano
Adam Deadmarsh
Theo Fleury
Teemu Selanne
Mario Lemieux
Alexi Yashin
Brendan Shanahan
Mats Sundin
Ted Donato
Mark Recchi
Dino Ciccarelli

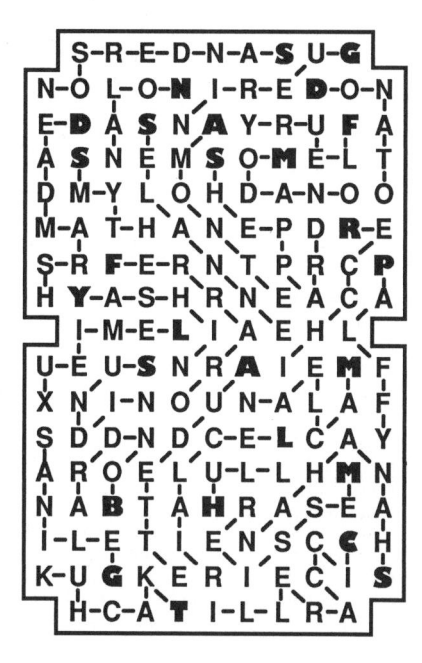

Brett Hull
Mark Messier
Keith Tkachuk
Donald Audette
Zigmund Palffy
John LeClair
Bill Guerin
Tony Amonte
Owen Nolan
Geoff Sanderson
Ryan Smyth
Peter Bronda
Martin Gelinas

GAME 5: EVOLUTION OF A RECORD

Part 1

Year	Career Goals	Scoring Leaders
1919–20	146	Joe Malone
1922–23	246	Cy Denneny
1933–34	270	Howie Morenz
1936–37	324	Nels Stewart
1951–52	544	Maurice Richard
1962–63	801	Gordie Howe
1993–94	863	Wayne Gretzky

The bogus name is Phil Esposito, who never surpassed Howe's record of 801 goals. The bogus number is 301.

Part 2

Year	Career Points	Point Leaders
1920–21	100	Joe Malone
1928–29	315	Cy Denneny
1931–32	467	Howie Morenz
1938–39	515	Nels Stewart
1944–45	528	Syd Howe
1946–47	548	Bill Cowley
1951–52	610	Elmer Lach
1953–54	946	Maurice Richard
1959–60	1,850	Gordie Howe
1988–89	2,705	Wayne Gretzky

The bogus name is Stan Mikita. Mikita never equalled Howe's record of 1,850 points. The bogus number is 2,135.

THE GOAL SCORERS

GAME 6: THE PINWHEEL PUZZLE

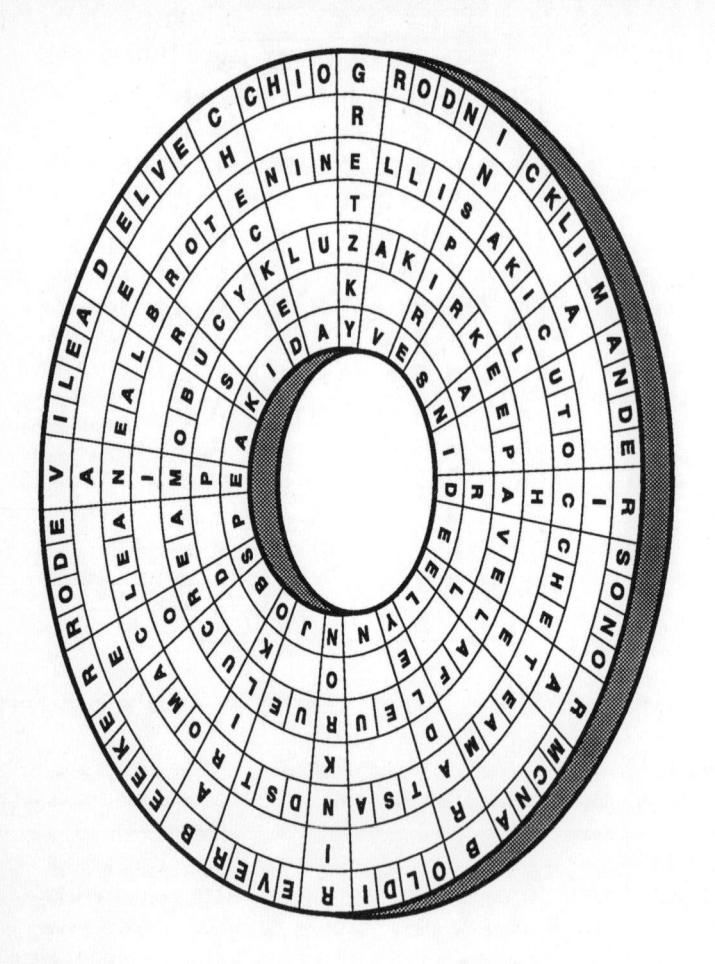

GAME 7: GAMES-PLAYED LEADERS

So who is the NHL's games-played leader after Gordie Howe? Once all the words in the puzzle are circled and the remaining letters joined in descending order, it's Alex Delvecchio. Howe played in 1,767 games during 26 seasons with Detroit and Hartford, from 1946–47 to 1979–80; Delvecchio played 24 seasons and 1,549 games, all with the Red Wings, from 1950–51 to 1973–74.

GAME 8: OLD-TIMER TOTALS

Player	Years	GP	G	A	PTS	PIM
1. Mike Bossy	10	752	573	553	1,126	210
2. Babe Dye	11	269	202	42	243	205
3. Bobby Orr	12	657	270	645	915	953
4. Steve Shutt	13	930	424	393	817	410
5. Howie Morenz	14	550	270	197	467	563
6. Bobby Clarke	15	1,144	358	852	1,210	1,453
7. Bobby Hull	16	1,063	610	560	1,170	640
8. Brad Park	17	1,113	213	683	896	1,429
9. Rod Gilbert	18	1,065	406	615	1,021	508
10. Don Marshall	19	1,176	265	324	589	127
11. Doug Harvey	20	1,113	88	452	540	1,216
12. Jean Ratelle	21	1,281	491	776	1,267	276
13. Dean Prentice	22	1,378	391	469	863	484
14. Johnny Bucyk	23	1,540	556	813	1,369	497
15. Tim Horton	24	1,446	115	403	518	1,611
16. Gordie Howe	26	1,767	801	1,049	1,846	1,675

ABOUT THE AUTHOR

Don Weekes is a TV producer and writer in Montreal. He recently produced the documentary *Passing the Torch*, the story of the building of Molson Centre. This is his tenth hockey trivia book and his third in the *Old-Time Hockey Trivia* series.

ACKNOWLEDGEMENTS

The author gratefully acknowledges the cooperation of Jean Béliveau and hockey photographer Harold Barkley; the help of the Public Relations department at the Philadelphia Flyers Hockey Club; Steve Dryden at *The Hockey News*; Phil Pritchard and Craig Campbell at the Hockey Hall of Fame; the staff at the McLennan-Redpath Library of McGill University; Rob Sanders and Robert Clements at Greystone Books; the many hockey writers and broadcasters who have made the game better through their own work; as well as my wife Caroline van Vlaardingen, editors Kerry Banks and Anne Rose, fact checker Allen Bishop, graphic artist Ivor Tiltin and puzzle designer Adrian van Vlaardingen.

PHOTO CREDITS

Harold H. Barkley: Brett Hull page 7; Jean Béliveau private collection: Jean Béliveau page 7; Robert B. Shaver: page 12; Imperial Oil-Turofsky/Hall of Fame archives: pages 34, 40; Bill Galloway: pages 80, 119; Jeff Goode: page 117; Graphic Artists/Hall of Fame archives: page 123; Frank Prazak/Hall of Fame archives: page 133
All other photos: Hockey Hall of Fame archives